A Life Worth Living

Wishing You
Good Things!
Bill Giruzzi

A Life Worth Living

William F. Giruzzi

Two Harbors Press
212 3rd Avenue North, Suite 570
Minneapolis, MN 55401
612.455.2293
www.TwoHarborsPress.com

ISBN - 978-1-935097-30-3
ISBN - 1-935097-30-x
LCCN - 2008911551

Book sales for North America and international:
Itasca Books, 3501 Highway 100 South, Suite 220
Minneapolis, MN 55416
Phone: 952.345.4488 (toll free 1.800.901.3480)
Fax: 952.920.0541; email to orders@itascabooks.com

Cover Design by Alan Pranke
Typeset by Peggy LeTrent

Printed in the United States of America

Contents

Acknowledgement

If I have seen further, it is by standing on the shoulders of giants.
—Sir Isaac Newton

I have wanted to write a book for years. I tried on many occasions but nothing came. Then, one day in late fall 2004, I sat down at my computer and just started writing. I couldn't stop; I guess I must have been ready. Funny thing is, while the essence of that first draft is in here somewhere, that version seems a distant memory. I probably still have people in my life who won't believe the book is finished until they are holding it in their hands. I don't know what the problem is—I've only finished it about thirty times, give or take a few.

This acknowledgement is to those people who always believed in me.

First, my thanks to those who took the time to read various versions and provide me with valuable feedback. Thank you to Marie Barnes, Rick and Elaine Conety, Maury and Kim Bouchard, John McCabe, Christine Lenney, and Judith Glaser. Also, special thanks to Rosemary Naftalis for providing her artistic talents. Thanks, Romary!

Next, thanks to Mark Meritt, my friend since college. Thanks for the wonderful editing job and for the patience you displayed in letting me find and follow my pathway. Thanks for our "big fat conversation" and for sticking through it with me to get to the other side. It was transformational. The leadership you provided is a true testament to your growth and development as a new mind.

Thanks to my best friend, Tommasino Salvatore Conte. I know it seems rather formal to use a full name for a best friend, but then you'd have to know Tommasino Salvatore Conte to appreciate why he will be tickled pink to see his full name in print in all its glory (although he still will razz me because I didn't use a different font to make it stand out). Tom, thank you for always being there, for your advice and insight, for your friendship, and for being able to see into my heart and be friend enough to say, "It's not done. You haven't said what there is *for you* to say yet."

Thanks to my family, who supported me throughout my life: Pam, for always making me laugh; Rocco, for being my big brother. Mom and Dad, what can I say? Mom, you taught me to nurture others. Dad, you taught me to innovate and to be of service to others. Thank you both for your endless hours of work and devotion to give me every opportunity in life and for always being proud as I followed my own pathway.

To Toby, my Maltese puppy, thank you for showing me what true joy is and for teaching me to be present in life.

Finally, to Lisa, my wife, thank you for your love. Thank you for always believing in me. Thank you for thinking that every version was miles above the last. Mostly though, thank you for the best conversations I've had in my life. I love you.

These are some of my giants, and it's on their shoulders that I offer this book to you.

Introduction

The purpose of this book is broad and bold: This book is about a new vision for human beings and our place in the world. This book is about the purpose of our lives. This book is about a new paradigm.

Paradigm? People sometimes cringe and stop listening when they hear the word paradigm. While it may sound "neo-business," a paradigm is simply a set of assumptions or concepts that constitute a way of viewing reality. Thus, Newtonian physics is a paradigm. Quantum physics is a paradigm. The Copernican view of the universe, the Ptolemaic view, the Freudian view of psychology, the Jungian—all of these are paradigms. They all represent a set of concepts and assumptions that constitute a way of viewing and understanding what's happening in reality. Still, the term "paradigm" has become overused and misunderstood. This has led some to mistrust the term. Some believe it implies that something isn't actually happening out here in the "real world"; that "it's all in your head." This is not the case. An apple really does fall from a tree; there really is an electromagnetic wave making it to your television that results in a picture. If you smash your car into a wall, there will be consequences.

The assumptions of quantum physics, however, do make something different available to physicists than the assumptions of Newtonian physics. Newtonian physics led to one level of understanding of how the universe works, while quantum physics is leading to a deeper level of understanding. Each has created a different view of what's happening in reality.

Here's a simple example to further demonstrate the idea of a paradigm. Below, there are two points—A and B—drawn in Figure 1. Draw this diagram on a separate sheet of paper and then draw a connecting line between points A and B.

Fig. 1

If you are like most people who have completed this exercise, you connected points A and B with a straight line, as illustrated in Figure 2.

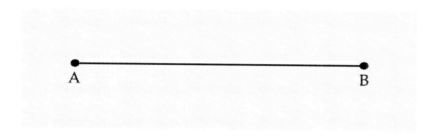

Fig. 2

Connecting the points with a straight line likely was automatic. You probably didn't even stop to consider that you could have connected them differently. In fact, you may have imagined a straight line between the two points, even before seeing the instruction to connect them. If you think about it, there are an infinite number of ways to connect points A and B other than with a straight line.[1]

It's not that your assumption—in this case, something like "the shortest distance between two points is a straight line"— isn't true; it's that in making the choice to draw a straight line between points A and B, you likely were not even aware you were being guided by an underlying assumption. *Paradigms are so powerful that they cause people to take particular actions without realizing an assumption is guiding—even dictating or limiting—their actions.* Thus, when directed to connect the points, most people automatically do so with a straight line. That's the power of a paradigm.

Paradigms, however, are not just formal models found in physics and math. Paradigms influence how we think about

---

1. This is especially true if you consider three-dimensional pathways (e.g., pathways coming out of the book). For instance, imagine a line coming out of the book at point A, straight toward your face, doing a circle around your head, and then landing back on the book at point B. Even if we just consider two-dimensional pathways, there are still many more that just a straight line.

and live every aspect of our lives. There are paradigms that influence how we are in our intimate relationships, how we act as parents, how we choose a mate, and how we work. There is a paradigm of how to live.

Consider the following question: Which do you think is more likely to happen? Someday we will be living on Mars, or someday we will develop a way of living on this planet where all people are fulfilled. Everyone to whom I've posed this question has answered, without fail, that it is more likely that we will one day live on Mars. People have such a strong faith and belief in our ability to invent things, to invent technology, and to discover the knowledge required for us to invent these innovations. But when it comes to discovering knowledge of how people can live fulfilling, healthy, happy lives, people tend to throw their hands up in frustration and helplessness. "There is no such knowledge. People are all so different; how could there be knowledge applicable to all?" Therein lies the limitation of the paradigm in which we live. We've come to believe that because we don't have the knowledge of how to live in a way that works for all people, that knowledge doesn't exist. I am not talking about a utopia where there is no tragedy or no disagreement; where nothing bad happens and where everyone is always nice to each other. I am talking about a way to live where real people are living real lives in a more fulfilling way.

I am talking about a life worth living.

Are *you* living a life worth living?

Each of us has to answer that question for ourselves, and if your answer is "Yes, I am," you'll get no argument from me. The way you live is not some horrible atrocity from which I am going to save you. If your answer, however, is "No, I am not," I will caution you right now that this book will not give you a laundry list of things to do to make your life better. This book aims to do something more powerful than that. This book is going to cause you to see life—to see *your* life—in a differ-

4

ent light. It's going to give you a different view of life. Now, if you think this book should do more than that, I invite you to recall my simple "A to B" exercise. The number of pathways from A to B is limitless, yet your action likely was limited to one quick, automatic choice. This limitation did not exist in reality; it existed only in your mind. These same limitations of mind exist in how you live your life. Now, are the pathways limitless from where you are to where you want to be? I don't know, but there are certainly more than you perceive. If you are suffering, struggling, or otherwise frustrated by trying to live a fulfilling life—a life worth living—you are doing so unnecessarily.

And so, it is not necessary for me to give you new actions; it is only necessary for you to see. By the end of this book, you'll have a new vision of life, and you'll have a new vision of yourself.

Life is a wonder, and it's time for you to see.

CHAPTER 1

Work: A Cultural Phenomenon

If someone were asked to describe our way of life, he or she likely would say something like the following:

> We are born, and we grow up. At around age five, we start going to school, where we learn things to prepare us for life. About twelve years later, we graduate high school, and some of us move right into the work force. Others go on to college, first as an undergraduate and then, for some, continuing on to get a master's degree or beyond. At some point we find work — we provide services and receive a paycheck in return — because we all need money to live — to pay for food and shelter and to take care of ourselves. We work at our jobs for about thirty to forty years, with two weeks vacation per year and weekends off. At some point we retire, at which time we hope that we have saved enough money to live well for the rest of our lives. We just try to enjoy the rest of our lives.

Clearly, the above statement doesn't begin to capture the complexity of our way of life; it doesn't address government, religion, relationships, or war. It makes no reference to political systems, economic systems, transportation systems, or technology. The list could go on, but while there certainly is more to our way of life, working or preparing ourselves to work is how we spend most of our waking hours. Life requires us to make a living, and so work is a defining characteristic of any way of life. We refer to some of our ancestors as hunter-gatherers or farmers because of the way they made a living. Today, working in business defines our way of life.

We each have our own personal experiences with work; some of us love our work, but many us don't love our work—or even like it. The Gallup Organization conducted a study that gives us an idea of how many Americans enjoy the work they do. Gallup found that only 29% of U.S. workers are engaged in their work. Of the remaining 71%, 55% are not engaged in their work, and 16% are actively disengaged. Curt Coffman, co-author of *First Break All the Rules: What the World's Greatest Managers Do Differently* and consultant for the Gallup Organization, described the distinction of being engaged, not engaged, or actively disengaged from work in the following way:

> The "engaged" employees are builders. They use their talents, develop productive relationships, and multiply their effectiveness through those relationships. They perform at consistently high levels. They drive innovation and move their organization forward. The employees that are "not engaged" aren't necessarily negative or positive about their company. They basically take a wait-and-see attitude toward their job, their employer, and their coworkers. They hang back and don't commit themselves.
>
> This brings us to the "actively disengaged" employees—the "cave dwellers." They're "**C**onsistently **A**gainst **V**irtually **E**verything." We've all worked with an actively disengaged employee who is not just unhappy at work; he *acts out* that unhappiness. Every day, actively disengaged employees tear down what their engaged coworkers are building.[1]

The next time you go to work, stop and look around, and consider that there are only three people out of ten who are truly engaged in their work. The rest are just going through the motions. Certainly, most of them are getting their work done, but they are not engaged. If you ask them what they are look-

---

1. "The High Cost of Disengaged Employees: There are 'cave dwellers' in your ranks, and they're hurting your company," *Gallup Management Journal*, April 15, 2002.

ing forward to, chances are they are simply living for the next reprieve—the next break, lunch, five o'clock, the weekend, or the next vacation. The intention here is not to debate your personal experience of work, but remember: 71% of people are not engaged in or are actively disengaged from their work. That's a cultural phenomenon. Statistics aside, this phenomenon is powerfully captured in three well-known phrases: Monday morning blues, Wednesday hump day, and "Thank God it's Friday!"

Monday morning blues—the drudgery begins. My wife, Lisa, was once on an elevator when a man entered, looking depressed. She greeted him with "How are you?" He looked at her pitifully and sighed, "It's Monday." My wife sighed herself, a bit deflated. If this question and answer had taken place in a courtroom, one might expect that opposing counsel would have jumped up and shouted, "Objection! Non-responsive to the question!" In life, though, the answer "It's Monday" to the question "How are you?" carries a very clear meaning, one that is almost akin to "It's time to go back to prison and continue serving my sentence." Even if you are one of the lucky ones who doesn't personally experience Monday morning blues, you still understand what the phrase means, and chances are you could spot a case of Monday morning blues just as easily as you could spot a case of chickenpox.

Then, there's Wednesday hump day. By the time Wednesday rolls around, you have had sufficient time to separate yourself from the fun and freedom of the weekend. You are thick in the middle of the workweek. You can begin to see the light at the end of the tunnel—the light of the weekend, of freedom. By the time Wednesday is over, 60% of the workweek will be behind you.

Then, finally, it's here—the magical day has arrived. It's dress-down day. It's Friday. Yes, there is still work to be done, but it's just one day—you can do one day. There is a buzz of excitement in the air. People are working, but you can feel a different energy in the office. Finally, the clock hits five o'clock, and you burst through the doors. You stop and look up at the heavens, and you shout, "Thank God it's Friday!" You are on a forty-eight-hour furlough. You are free to do exactly what you want to do, when you want to do it.

Does this sound at all insane to you? I've always found it intriguing that although people complain about work—they complain about having to go to work, they complain about their supervisors, they complain about management—typically, the only things they ever request to make things better are things that have nothing to do with the work itself. People will ask for an increase in salary, more vacation time, better benefits—things that impact the quality of life *outside* of work—but they don't seem to demand that the work itself be more fulfilling; that would be a change that would really impact their quality of life. Certainly money, vacation time, and other benefits are important and impact the quality of our lives, but even when we acquire these things, we often continue to dread the experience of work.

Every day, people trade their time, their passion, their fulfillment, and their heart for a paycheck and benefits. They trade fulfillment now for the promise of fulfillment in the future. Life always seems to be about the next weekend, the next vacation, and finally, if you are lucky enough to live that long, retirement. Life is not about living; it's about surviving—surviving long enough to really live.

Does this all sound insane now?

The insanity of it all made me wonder: "What could possibly be going on that people would make such a trade?" I've concluded that it is actually not a trade at all. A trade implies a conscious decision to give up something in exchange for something else. In my mind, there is only one reason why people would give up their passion and fulfillment in exchange for thirty to forty years of drudgery and security.

They must have felt there was no choice at all.

QUESTIONS FOR FURTHER DISCOVERY

NOTE: At the end of each chapter, I've included questions to help you more fully explore the ideas in this book. Answering these questions is not the point of this book; use them or don't use them. It's possible to not answer these questions and get the value from this book, and it's possible to answer these questions and not get the value. Don't misunderstand—these questions can be extremely powerful and may, in fact, be key to helping you get the value of this book. They simply are not *necessary*, nor is it the point that you be able to answer them. In short, use them as you see fit.

1. What other things would you include to describe our way of life?

2. It's easy to say that there are different ways of life around the world because there are different cultures, governments, etc. What if you take the point of view that they are all different expressions of the same way of life? How does that change how you think about it? What is *the* way of life that is represented in all of the different expressions?

3. What are the things you demand at work? What are the things that would really make a difference in your quality of life? Are these things the same?

4. "There's life and then there's work." We talk about balancing work and life. Does that seem odd to you? Work is a part of life, and yet we divided the line in a place where it can't be divided. What does this say about how we perceive life, work, and ourselves?

CHAPTER 2

It's All Made Up

How did life come to be this way? Have you ever thought about that? How did we end up with our particular way of life? How did we end up working in business? Throughout history, people have attempted to gain some insight into how to live a better life. We have examined life from many different perspectives. From a historical perspective, we have looked at the events of our past to understand why things happen as they do and to see if we can learn anything about ourselves. Despite the wisdom of philosopher George Santayana, who noted "Those who do not learn from history are doomed to repeat it," sometimes it seems we have not learned much from history when we examine the state of the world—and even our own lives.

From a moral perspective, we ask whether the actions or events of our past were right or wrong. From a philosophical perspective, we have tried to glean some understanding of who we are and to make some sense of our lives. "What is the meaning of life?" we have asked. "Why are we here?" Despite endless inquiries and the many different answers these perspectives have given us, it seems we not only don't know how to live a better life, but we are not even sure why or how we ended up with this way of life.

To demonstrate, consider the following dialogue between a young girl named Sandy and her mother:

Sandy: Mommy, why don't you and Daddy and I spend the whole day together all the time? Some days we do, but on other days, we don't.

Mom: Well, honey, we spend the whole day together on the weekend—that's Saturday and Sunday. That's when most families get to spend time together. It's the most important time.

Sandy: Why can't we spend the other days together, too?

Mom: Because on those other days, Daddy and I have to go to work.

Sandy: Why, Mommy?

Mom: Mommy and Daddy go to work so that we can earn money. You know we live in this nice house, and you have nice clothes and wonderful toys. Our work gives us money so we can buy these nice things.

Sandy: I like living here, and I love my toys. But why do you and Daddy go to work so much?

Mom: We work five days. Some people do work less, and some work more, but most work five days each week.

Sandy: But you and Daddy stay at home with me only on … the weekend.

Mom: That's right. We stay home on two days.

Sandy: But two isn't as many as five.

Mom: Yes, that's right.

Sandy: But why don't you work for two days and stay home with me for five days?

Mom: Because then we wouldn't make enough money for us to live in this nice house.

Sandy: Why not? You said being together was the most important thing.

Mom: Yes, it is.

Sandy: Then why don't you get paid the same but only work for two days?

Mom: That's just not the way things work. We work five days a week and have two days off.

Sandy: But *why?*

Mom: I don't know why exactly, honey. *It's just the way it is.*

You may be able to relate to Sandy's mom. How do you explain to a young child the complexities of why you choose to spend time working instead of spending time with her—especially when you don't really know the answer yourself? There is undoubtedly someone who could answer Sandy's question in detail—"In a free market economy, salaries are set by ... and we need to work five days because ..."—but no matter how sound an answer, Sandy (or any other child) could still persist with an unending barrage of "why." Why is it this way? Intellectually, we know there's an answer. We know that all of this—the way we live—didn't just happen. We're intelligent, capable people, yet when it comes to the things most important to us, the best answer most of us have come up with—just like Sandy's mom—is "It's just the way it is."

Our quest to find more academic or more complex answers has led us to ignore one inescapable truth: It's all made up. Far from being "just the way it is," our way of life and business and all the rest has resulted from the very complex yet simple process of design. The process is simple in that it basically involves choice mixed with chance. It is complex in the sheer number of choices involved in the process. Our way of life is neither an immutable law of nature nor ordained by a supreme being; it is the result of choices made, consciously and unconsciously, by people.

"It's all made up." I can appreciate why this statement sounds a little "out there," but here's what I mean: Consider the timeline of the existence of human beings. Whatever your beliefs regarding how humans arrived on this planet, at some point we arrived. When we arrived there were no cars, no airplanes, no skyscrapers, no houses—none of the man-made things that exist today. There also were no ways of life; there wasn't hunting and gathering, farming, or business. There wasn't even the idea of any of these things. Now, all of these things—cars, planes, skyscrapers, and business—do in fact exist, so at some point between when people arrived on this planet and today, all of these things *were created and designed.*

To be precise, though, when I say that our way of life was created and designed, I am not saying that someone in our past woke up one morning and said to himself, "I'm going to invent a way of life today." Just like everything created by people, our way of life came about by a very complex and chaotic process of experimentation and choice that was done by many people who were just being creative with the knowledge they had available to them. Its creation was not an event that can be measured in a day, a year, or even a decade. It was a process that occurred over the course of many years.

Why, though, is this perspective of design so important? What does design teach us that history, morals, and philosophy fail to teach? Let me illustrate that importance with an example: Imagine that Sandy has asked me to build a wagon. I've never made a wagon, but I'm going to try to make it extra-special for Sandy. After careful deliberation, I decide on the following design for the wagon:

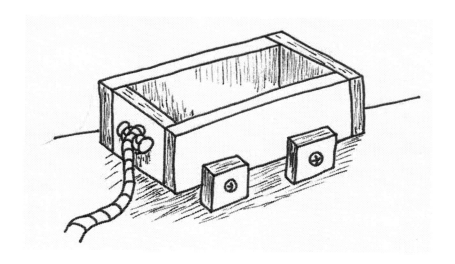

Thereafter, I spend months carefully crafting this wagon, although its obvious design flaw goes unnoticed. Finally, my wagon is complete. I proudly present the wagon to Sandy, who gleefully grabs the rope handle and attempts to pull the wagon—only to discover the obvious: square wheels don't roll! At that moment, the flaw in the design is not a philosophical concern; it's a very practical concern.

Similarly, the principles and assumptions that make up our way of life are firmly entrenched in the practical, not the philosophical, regardless of how long ago the choices were made. There are only two differences between the design choice for the wagon and the design choices for our way of life:

1. The level of complexity in the design of our way of life is much greater than the level of complexity in the design of a wagon.

2. The time between creating the design and use of the wagon was short enough that I could easily observe the practical impact of the design. The time between when our way of life was created and the effect of the design, however, spans many years, which makes it more difficult to see the connection.

Despite the disparate time lag in cause and effect, we are living today with the very practical consequences of a design that was invented long before those of us who are alive today arrived on this planet. I am not saying the design of our way of life is so flawed that—much like my square-wheeled wagon—it didn't take us anywhere. In fact, I am not saying that the design is flawed at all; nevertheless, the design, like anything that is designed, has consequences—good and bad, intended and unintended.

This, though, was not the explanation that we were taught. This is not the explanation we were given when our parents left Monday morning to go to work, or when we were eventually shuffled off to school, or whenever we asked a question that an adult couldn't answer about how we live. We learned the messages of our culture just as Sandy did: "This is how people live"; "This is all there is"; and "It's just the way it is." I am asking you to consider that lack of fulfillment is not an individual phenomenon; instead, lack of fulfillment is a naturally occurring result that is consistent with the design of our way of life. Lack of fulfillment is by design. All of it is by design. As I said, "It's all made up." Perhaps history, morals, and philosophy have reached their limit in terms of the answers they can provide. Nevertheless, there are new answers to be found in the realm of design.

QUESTIONS FOR FURTHER DISCOVERY

1. What would you tell Sandy? Do you think you could satisfy her questions?

2. Think about your life. Where is your life "just the way it is"? How would that change if you considered that your life is an outcome of design?

3. Many experience burden when they think of their life as their responsibility or a result of their choices. Do you experience burden or freedom? If burden, how would you have to think about responsibility differently in order to experience freedom? What beliefs do you have associated with responsibility that makes it feel like a burden?

4. "It's all made up." Do you think there is a fundamental belief held today that where we ended up today is where we were supposed to end up? Hunter-gatherers toiled. Peasants toiled. Farmers toiled. All of our ancestors toiled so we could get here today. It's not just the way it is; *it's the way it's supposed to be,* isn't it? What other fundamental beliefs do we hold about our way of life?

CHAPTER 3

Building Blocks

Before we can delve more deeply into the design of our way of life, we must more closely examine two basic concepts—two building blocks—of design. The first is cause and effect.

CAUSE AND EFFECT

In the realm of design, this notion of cause and effect is a critical concept. My intent is to deepen your awareness of how this process operates in our lives. To that end, I am going to tell you a story of how a man shifted from hunting and gathering to farming. My purpose is to distinguish how cause and effect plays a part in developing ways of living; it is not intended to be a historically accurate (or even fully plausible) account of how humans made the transition. Rather, I've taken a very complex process and simplified it by way of example:

> *There once was a man named Neo. Neo lived a simple life, as he explored the earth. If he was hungry, he ate berries from the bushes and all types of fruit from the trees. If he saw a fox or a deer and was hungry, he killed and ate it. Otherwise, he walked and played and swam and ran and rested. One day, when Neo was*

out walking, he stepped into a hole and sprained his ankle. The sprain was so bad that he couldn't play and run as he usually did. In fact, he could barely walk. Luckily, Neo was in the midst of a very large field of berries, so he didn't have to worry about food. Many days and nights passed as Neo's ankle healed. During that time, Neo had time to sit and observe the world around him. He noticed that the berries he ate came from a bush, and the bush came out of the ground. He began to wonder where that bush had come from. As he sat there, he dug with his hands to see what lay beneath the ground, but there was nothing there. No answers. Neo's ankle eventually healed, and he moved on. He went back to walking and running and eating and playing, but now Neo also wondered where the berries had come from. So, as he did all the things he usually did each day, Neo also began to learn some things about how the berries grew.

One night a terrible storm came, and Neo needed to find some shelter. He came across a cave and was grateful for the protection from the wind and the rain. When morning came, Neo awoke and saw that the sun was shining. He ran from the cave to discover that he had found a very wonderful place. From where he stood, he could see a nice pond to swim in. There were ample bushes filled with berries; there were fields of grass for him to run in; and there was the protection of this cave. Neo thought to himself, "I think I'll stay here a while." So Neo ate and he ran and swam and played and walked, and he continued to think about the berries.

Neo hadn't ventured out too far in quite a long time; he liked it so much here. At one point, though, it occurred to him that the bushes filled with berries were becoming bare, and soon he would need to find some food. This created a dilemma for Neo, because he loved it here so much. Nevertheless, he would either need to move, or he would need to find some other way to get food. "Perhaps if I could grow some berry bushes myself," he thought, "then I wouldn't have to leave." So he tried and tried, until one day he did it. He grew his very own berry bush. He planted many bushes so that he would never have to leave this wonderful place.

But then one day he began to realize that he was becoming tired of berries. In his journeys, he used to find apples and pears and corn and so many other types of food to eat, as well as an occasional fox or rabbit, too. He longed for those other types of food, and thus he was once again faced with a dilemma: should he move on or should he stay? He began to wonder, "If I could grow berries, perhaps I could grow other types of food on this land."

And then time passed ...

Of course, this story is not intended to give you an accurate historical perspective (or even a fully plausible explanation) on how the transition was made from hunting and gathering to farming as a way of life. It's simply to demonstrate the mechanism of cause and effect in the process of design. Some of the causes were simply the result of chance—Neo's sprained ankle and his need for protection from the storm were the result of chance. One of the effects of his sprained ankle was that Neo took the time to observe his world. This brought his natural curiosity alive and gave him a question to engage his thinking. Certainly it was chance that brought Neo to find the particular cave, but it was conscious choice that made him decide to stay. An unintended effect was the reduction of his food supply. When he tied himself to a set geographic location, he tied himself to the food supply of that location. Not only was this effect unintended, but Neo may have very likely not even made the connection between his decision to stay and the reduction of the food source. Instead, he might have wondered,

"What's the problem with these bushes?" Unlike the short time lag between design choice (cause) and effect that occurred with my square-wheeled wagon, which allowed us to make the connection between cause and effect, Neo likely did not make the connection between his choice of lifestyle (design) and the effect of that lifestyle. You and I are able to see the link, but the only difference between our way of life and Neo's is that the choices that make up our way of life were made long ago and have resulted in such a high level of complexity that we can no longer see the causes from the effects.

In fact, effects become the cause of our next choice. Neo decided to stay at the cave because he liked it there. The effect of this choice was that it depleted his food source. This effect—the depleted food source—became the cause of his need to make the choice whether to stay or to go. This decision was more difficult because he now liked it there. Perhaps he liked not having to move around all the time. He was becoming accustomed to his lifestyle. This was the result of a culmination of causes—a storm, his increased knowledge, and his choice to stay at the cave. Of course, the level of complexity in our lives today is much greater. We are dealing with the effects of choices that were made hundreds, even thousands, of years ago.

Now, to be fair, we don't know the real cause of Neo's depleted food source. It could have had absolutely nothing to do with Neo's decision to stay at his cave, but still, the ultimate tenet of design is that every cause has an effect, and *every choice has an effect. Every choice we make both creates and limits opportunities that are available to us.* For Neo, the effect of his choices wasn't too limiting—Neo could have easily picked up and moved. Our choices seem to be more limited. A choice can limit opportunities, but we can always make another choice. If we can choose differently, however, then why does it seem like choices regarding our way of life, regarding our lives, seem to be written in stone? The reason for this perceived limitation is brought about by the other building block of design known as structure.

STRUCTURE

In the realm of design, every thought or idea on which one takes action leads to a "thing" in life. For example, if you decide to bake a cake, you take certain actions that use your knowledge of how to bake, and the result is the structure: cake. You have transformed the idea to a physical structure.

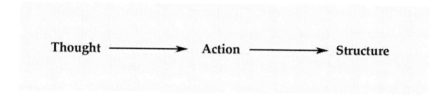

Structure is not just the physical manifestation of your idea; structure also has a mental aspect—this is what I have been referring to as a paradigm. Let's take the example of a car. We would have:

Thought   ⟶   Action   ⟶   Structure
"Something motorized   "Car"
to move from A to B"

Obviously, the process of creating a car is much more complex than the process of baking a cake. When the automobile was invented, every part of it went through its own creation process. The parts were created and put together to create the "whole" car. After the car was invented, there was the physical manifestation of the car, but there also was a mental structure, or paradigm "car," that was created.

If I asked the average person to describe a car, he likely would say that it has four wheels, two or four doors, an engine that propels it forward, brakes that make it stop, a body that is in some particular shape, a steering wheel, ignition, gear shifter, and so on. Even if you have no idea what is happening under the hood, you could still give a pretty good description of a car. The paradigm "car" has structure to it that is as real to us as the physical car's frame and doors and windshield. While we could imagine adding heat, air conditioning, heated seats, a stereo system, and other innovations to the basic design of a car to make a car ride more pleasurable, how about imagining a car with no brakes? What if, instead of brakes, we added an engine that utilized reverse propulsion to stop the car? Now, your response might be "Why would we bother doing that? Brakes work fine." I am not suggesting that we change the design; I am simply saying that there is mental structure around a car that goes beyond the physical manifestation of the car. There is a paradigm "car" that keeps us from thinking about a car in any other way unless and until there is a need for it.

Additionally, the physical structure that is created extends beyond the car itself. We have built an entire way of life around this one invention. We developed a complex system of roads. We built our cities and suburbs around the car. We have government entities that are responsible for building and maintaining our roads. And don't forget the car industry itself. Even if using a reverse propulsion engine made a better car, there would be resistance to eliminating brakes, because an entire industry would be wiped out if brakes were eliminated.

Suppose we wanted to eliminate cars from our lives altogether; the structure that has resulted from this one invention is so overwhelming that it would seem impossible to eliminate it. This is just one layer of the complexity of our world that was created by one structure: the car. The point is we know we live in a complex world, but we are not fully cognizant of the fact that we created all of it. This complex world didn't just happen; *we created a complex world to live in*. We created the causes and the effects. We designed our own square-wheeled wagon and are now living with the impact.

Still, it seems impossible that we could change it in some way to really make a difference in the quality of our lives. What aspect of our way of life could we change to make things better? In Neo's scenario, it would be easy for him to walk away from his way of life because there was not much structure—physical or mental—to it. If we were to try to walk away from our way of life, however, where would we go to permanently get away? Even if we could get away from the physical structure we've created, we carry the mental structure, the paradigm of how to live, with us wherever we go. Here's the key to it all:

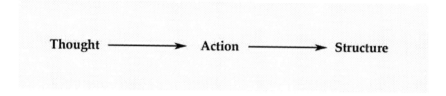

All of our structure, every bit of it, is the result of an idea, of thought. Of course, we can't just make the physical structures in our world disappear by erasing them from our minds, but the limitation in our ability to create is not real. It's an illusion created by the massive physical and mental structure we've created. To reveal the illusion, the next step is to explore one of the most dominant structures we've created: the paradigm of business.

QUESTIONS FOR FURTHER DISCOVERY

1. What effects are you living with today from the choices you made in the past?

2. What effects are you living with today from choices made by other people in the time before you were born?

3. What would you change about our way of life? What would be the intended or unintended impact of that change?

4. What choices made by our ancestors might not be perceived as "choice"? For example, do you think of the pursuit of mathematics as a choice?

CHAPTER 4

The Paradigm of Business

B usiness is highly complex, so while we won't look at every principle that makes up the paradigm of business, we will examine three of the most basic—principles so basic, in fact, that they likely won't be much of a revelation. As you read these principles, keep two things in mind: First, the overall objective is to reveal the limitation in thought that keeps us from making our lives better. Second, the obviousness of these principles does not change the fact that these principles are made up. These principles represent choices in how we designed business, and ultimately, they represent choices in the way in which people should live. Keep in mind, though, that you may not relate to these things as "choices." Relating to something as a choice is different from relating to it by thinking of it as "just the way it is." For example, we don't have any choice with respect to the law of gravity. We've found ways to fly, but we did so by obeying the laws of gravity, not by defying them. The law of gravity is something that's "just the way it is." But designing business so that we could make a living was just as much a choice as creating airplanes so we could fly. With that in mind, let's examine the paradigm of business.

I'd like you to think about the specific businesses you might find in any city. Some of the businesses might be Dunkin' Donuts, McDonald's, K-Mart, Best Buy, Mobil, your local pizza shop, the post office, your county department of social services, the courthouse, your dentist, and the Salvation Army. Now I ask you: "Why do they exist?" I don't mean this as a philosophical question but a realistic one: Why does Dunkin' Donuts exist? Why does McDonald's exist? Simply put, these two businesses exist to sell doughnuts or hamburgers. The post office exists to deliver mail. A dental practice exists to maintain the health of your teeth. Each of these organizations has a defined purpose, a reason to exist.

Principle #1: *Every business has a fundamental purpose, and that purpose is to provide particular products or services.*

This principle is integral to the way in which we think about business. The point is simply that we humans were the creators of an entity whose sole purpose is to provide products and services. We could have chosen to organize business with some other fundamental purpose—we could have decided that the fundamental purpose of every business was to provide jobs for people. Although part of the purpose of business is to provide jobs, it's certainly not the fundamental purpose or reason for a business to exist. For example, if the heads of Dunkin' Donuts one day said, "We're done. No more donuts," the jobs provided by Dunkin' Donuts would cease to exist. If consumers decided they would no longer buy any of Dunkin' Donuts' products, the business would cease to exist. Now, if the fundamental purpose of a particular business was to provide jobs rather than to provide products and services, then this change of purpose would lead any company to make different decisions about that company's future. Rather than decide which products or services to provide and then determine how many people the company would need to provide the product or service, the company instead would figure out the largest of number of people it could employ and then create products and services to keep that number employed. Would it make sense to organize business around such a purpose? The answer to that question is irrelevant—it didn't happen that way. The intention here is not to pass judgment on what we chose; the intention is only to distinguish that we chose. Organizing a business around providing a particular product or service was a choice. It was an invention. It was a creation of human beings.

To distinguish the next principle, imagine that we are starting a business—a travel agency—so we sit down and have a conversation about starting the agency and what would be involved. Now, think about that conversation and the types of issues we would discuss.

Here's a list of some of the possible issues that we might discuss as we begin to design our travel agency:

- How much money do we need to start our business?
- Do we have enough? If not, where are we going to get the money?
- Where will this business be located?
- What corporate structure will our business take?
- What are the demographics of the area where we are starting our agency?
- How are we going to market our service?
- Will we have a separate marketing department? If so, what resources will it need?
- Will we have a website?
- How many agents will we employ? Will we have in-house salaried agents or commissioned independent agents, or both?
- Who will hire the agents?
- Who will do the training of the agents?
- Will we rent or buy property to house our agency?
- What equipment will we need (desks, computers, fax machines, telephones, office supplies)?

In designing our travel agency, you'll notice that there are certain factors that we considered, while others were not considered. Here's a list of thoughts and questions that we did not consider:

- George Washington is on the one-dollar bill.
- In considering location, where should it be located to ensure good karma?
- The New York Yankees have won twenty-six World Series Championships.
- In considering office space, will it allow for adequate sunlight and control of the temperature to ensure that agents are always working at the optimal temperature to promote effectiveness?
- Some politicians are working to privatize Social Security.
- What model computer should we use to get the greatest efficiency out of the agents so they enjoy doing their work?
- How should the corporate structure be designed so that all employees are fulfilled and satisfied in their work?

You might be wondering, "What the heck do any of those things have to do with designing a business?" That's the point. When anything is designed—a car, a computer, a house, a business—there are factors that are considered and factors that are not. In designing a business, you are no more likely to consider what model computer will optimize the agents' enjoyment of their work than you are to consider the fact that George Washington is on the one-dollar bill. We have a particular focus when we design a business. And that focus is on meeting the needs of the business.

Principle #2: Every choice of design is made for one reason and one reason only—to fulfill the purpose of business.

Even if the purpose of our entity is charitable, our conversations still would involve how to best design the organization so that the organization would become a viable entity. This fundamental choice of focus has had—and continues to have—an effect on our lives. When we think of business, we think of it as an entity separate from ourselves, so when we design a business, we put the focus on meeting the needs of the business.

This begs the question: "Where *don't* we put the focus?" When business was designed, the focus wasn't on people. It wasn't designed with people in mind. It wasn't designed for people as producers. From the standpoint as consumers, business was designed to meet our every need. From the standpoint as producers, business was designed to incorporate and use people.

So what about people? In our travel agency, we need to plan for how many people we are going to hire, what qualifications we are looking for, among other issues. Once people are hired, from the CEO right down to the custodian, they are somehow organized to achieve the purpose of the business. Think for a moment: regardless of whether you've had a nice boss or a nasty boss; regardless of whether you have control issues or are easygoing; regardless of whether you work in a hierarchy or another business structure; there is a fundamental way in which people are organized and managed. Are people organized and managed by the color of their hair? Are they organized and managed by the size of their feet? Of course not.

> *Principle #3: In business, people are organized and managed by their function to achieve the purpose of the business.*

Your reaction might be, "How else would they be organized?" Again, that's the point. There are millions of ways people could have been organized (including the color of their hair or the size of their feet), but organizing by function was one choice. Today, however, this type of organizing does not seem like one choice in a million choices (including all the ridiculous choices). It is the *only* choice; it's the obvious choice. It's what? Yes, you've got it. "It's just the way it is."

Are you thinking that this all seems anticlimactic? Perhaps you're thinking, "Tell me something I don't know." Of course, you know these things all too well. Like aspects of any other paradigm, you know them to the exclusion of all other possibilities. You do know business has a defined purpose. You *do* know, in the deepest levels of your consciousness, that everything is done to fulfill the purpose of business, and everything else, including meeting the needs of people, is secondary. You *do* know that in business, people have functions, and people are organized and managed by their function. You know these things so well that you've forgotten that it was, at one point, all made up — and so you live with the effects.

And what about the effects? That's a question you'll have to answer for yourself. Are you one of the 29% engaged? Or do you fall into the other 71%? How does it feel to be used or thought of as nothing more than a function? How does it feel to know that if push came to shove, fulfilling the purpose of the business outweighs your needs? For some of us, these things are not a problem. Some of us are quite content to show up to work every day, perform our function, and find fulfillment. The point is that your experience of work, whatever it is, is not just the way it is. Your experience of work is by design. *Your experience of life is by design.*

"But," you may wonder, "what if people are lazy or fundamentally flawed in some way? Can we assume the flaw is in the design of business? Maybe work will never be a good experience for us and our behavior will always need to be regulated by the policies and procedures of business?" Actually, this is the crux of the matter — the fundamental limitation created by the thinking of the current paradigm: *Why is it that anything is flawed?*

QUESTIONS FOR FURTHER DISCOVERY

1. Can you think of some other fundamental principles that make up the design of business?

2. What effect does the design of business have on you?

3. We design experiences all the time—we create a solemn atmosphere for a funeral by our actions, our dress, etc. We plan weddings to design an experience of joy and celebration. Your moment-to-moment experience is designed as well. Reflect on how your experience, thoughts, and emotions are a product of design.

CHAPTER 5

"Is This It?"

So we have these basic principles that make up the paradigm of business:

> *Principle #1: Every business has a fundamental purpose and that purpose is to provide particular products or services.*
>
> *Principle #2: Every choice of design is done for one reason and one reason only — to fulfill the purpose of business.*
>
> *Principle #3: In business, people are organized and managed by their function to achieve the purpose of the business.*

Certainly again, these are not the only principles, but you should be able to easily identify these principles in the way we do business. Even the effects of how we live are not a mystery. "Monday morning blues" and the "rat race" are phrases that we know all too well, and these effects are just part of the package too, aren't they? They are part of the paradigm – part of "just the way it is." And what about how we try to deal with these effects? Isn't that part of the paradigm too? We do everything we can to combat the effects of the current paradigm. We seek to find balance in our lives. We hire consultants to come into our organizations to conduct change initiatives that are designed to make our organizations more effective by making organizational life better for people. Sometimes, it seems the more we try to change things, the more things stay the same. And yet with all this effort, there is something about it all that just doesn't seem to occur to us.

Consider design principle #3 above. The impact of this principle is that it establishes the nature of our relationships at work: function to function. Certainly when you go to work, you develop personal relationships, yet personal relationships are not the dominant type of relationship that exists in business. Thus, if you are an attorney in an insurance company, for example, people talk to you about legal matters. If you are a mailroom clerk, people talk to you about the delivery of the mail—the matters related to your function.

Take a few moments to imagine that you are writing a job description for a secretary, and list the functions of a secretary.

I've suggested this to many people and amazingly, every single one of them has neglected to list the most vital role of a secretary. Their lists generally include answering the phone, being the gatekeeper for the boss, typing correspondence, scheduling appointments, faxing correspondence, copying or taking dictation. (And I always get one wise guy who answers "Making the coffee.") I am astonished, though, that people have never, ever listed the most vital role of a secretary: *to come up with ideas that make or save the company millions of dollars.*

Are you astonished?

Relating function to function is not insignificant. Relating function to function dictates what we talk about with each other, how we see each other, and what we expect from each other. Consider these questions: Do secretaries not have ideas that could make or save millions of dollars for the company? Or do secretaries simply not contribute those ideas that could make or save millions of dollars for the company because of the prescribed definition of the duties of a secretary? When you walk into any place of work and see a secretary, do you have any expectation that he or she will have a million-dollar idea? Would you even think to ask if a secretary had such an idea?

If a secretary did have an idea, would you take it as seriously as an idea from a CEO or a senior manager? If you have a secretary, do you ask about anything other than the tasks related to that job? Do you ask for input on how your secretary can better perform the required function? All of us—whether it's the mailroom clerk, the janitor, the lawyer, the secretary, or the CEO—are squeezed by the world of definition.

Now, you might realize that you do relate function to function with the people at your place of work. Maybe you've even decided that tomorrow, you will try to relate to your coworkers more as human beings. Perhaps you're a manager with a secretary. Perhaps you tell yourself, "I'm going to bring Sally into my office, sit her down, and ask her if she has any ideas that might help our company." You might actually be surprised to find that Sally has many ideas, all of which are excellent. In fact, Sally may have a million-dollar idea. Of course, you may also find that you either disagree with Sally's ideas or that they just are not very good ideas. It's also possible that Sally will be caught off guard by your asking for her input. She may offer only a blank expression as she says hesitantly, "Umm ... none that I can think of." Sally may have been too busy typing letters, answering the phone, sending faxes, and making appointments for you to have had any ideas about the company. She hasn't had the time to think, much less be creative. But even if Sally had no ideas to offer, your asking her might cause her to start thinking about it, and if you continue to periodically check in with her, she eventually might have some ideas to share.

But then, how many times do you check in with her? Two times? Five times? Twelve times? How many times do you check in with her before you decide she really does not have any ideas to share, and so you stop asking her?

Think about the entire conversation that you might have with Sally. You get your thoughts together, and you call her into your office. Maybe you tell her that you've been reading this book, and you realized something about how people relate at work. You ask for her input. She says that she doesn't have anything to offer. You pause and then say, "Okay, well I'm glad we had this talk. Just wanted to check in. I'll try to ask you periodically, and if any thoughts come to mind, let me know. Can you grab me the McClellan file on your way out? Thanks." In that moment, you've returned to the customary, everyday function-to-function language of business. Back to the grind; back to getting the job done. This is why there is resistance to change. We are fighting the pull of a centuries-old river that is running in the opposite direction.

So why bother, when we are in this river? Shouldn't we just accept it?

Yes, we should. The thing that never occurs to us is to just *let it all be.*

Let it be.

The phrase "Let it be," has been misconstrued. People think of it as something you have to spend your whole life working to understand or achieve. People often don't realize that right now, in this moment, what you are doing more than anything else is letting things be. Right now, look at a chair or some other object. Do you have any emotional reaction to the chair? Unless it is a family heirloom or you've attached emotion to the chair, you likely don't have any emotional reaction to it. Until I asked you to look at it and brought it into your awareness, you probably barely took notice of the chair. It's just a chair. It's just there; it just is. You don't engage the chair. You don't become emotionally entangled with the chair. The chair is in the background of your perception, and you let it be. Even if you're sitting in the chair, you let it be.

This is also your relationship to most of the things and people you encounter as you live your life. You pass by hundreds of thousands of structures and people each day without giving them any thought. You just let them be.

And so, letting things be is not some mysterious phenomenon you have to spend your whole life trying to understand. Everything, with respect to our way of life, is the result of creation, including the effects that our way of life has on us. Business isn't just the way it is. Our way of life isn't just the way it is. It is that way, and like everything else, *it is that way by design.* Because we are always working to fix the effects of the current paradigm—either through self-improvement programs designed to fix us so that we are more effective in our lives, or by somehow fixing the design of business or some other structure so that it is better for people. Because we don't let it all be, it never seems to occur to us that *neither the design of our way of life nor people need fixing.*

For example, the purpose of business is exactly as we designed it—to provide particular products and services. As producers, the purpose of business is not to give us fulfilling lives. Business is efficiently designed to fulfill its purpose, except for one thing: us. We keep getting in the way. The fact that most of us need more from life than what business can provide is our problem, and we should focus on that problem instead of trying to fix business or ourselves so that our lives are more fulfilling. The only thing that business needs from us is what it is designed to need from us: to perform functions at peak performance. Business needs people to perform their functions with the same efficiency and reliability that we expect when we turn on the ignition or step on the gas pedal of a car.

This vision of business may seem awfully cold, but think of it this way: if a loved one is having surgery, are you concerned whether the doctor is enjoying her work? No, you want a doctor who is efficient and reliable, a master even, at producing the expected result—a successful surgery. Still, producing a result efficiently and reliably can be done with passion and creativity. The Chicago Bulls' Michael Jordan was highly efficient and reliable at producing results, and he certainly did so with passion and creativity. Most of us would love to find something in our lives to which we could give that much passion and produce that level of results.

So if our way of life doesn't have to change, if business doesn't have to change, and we don't have to change, how is anything supposed to change? Consider this: When the car was invented, did life change for people? Of course it did. And when the airplane was invented, did life change for people? Absolutely. We don't need to change anything about the design of our way of life, and we don't need to fix ourselves.

We just need to invent a new way to live.

Let me repeat that: we need to invent a new way to live, one that gives us more of what we really want, instead of trying to fix the way of life we've already created. If you are like most people, you probably have asked yourself, at one time or another, the ultimate cosmic question: "Is this it? Is this all there is?"

Well, I'm here to tell you that this isn't all there is. There is much, much more.

QUESTIONS FOR FURTHER DISCOVERY

1. What things do you want that our way of life gives you?

2. What things do you want that our way of life doesn't give you?

3. What is your reaction to inventing a new way of life? Do you think we can? What beliefs get in the way of seeing the possibility of creating a new way of life?

CHAPTER 6

Someday, the Sun Will Go Out

Our sun is approximately 4.5 billion years old. It is estimated that the sun has about 5 billion years left in its life. I once thought that Earth would survive until the sun burned out. Not so. It seems that as the sun continues to age, it will expand to about fifty times its present size, at which point it will engulf Mercury and incinerate Venus and Earth. As it cools, Earth (or at least, life as we know it) will be long gone.

No one knows if this will be the actual scenario. Earth could someday—whether it's one billion years from now or next year—be wiped out by a totally different means. Still, most people seem to be clear that their own time on the earth is limited. They know they have eighty to possibly one hundred years in their lifespan. They may not always be present to their mortality, but they certainly do not delude themselves that they will live forever. The way they think about Earth's life is another story.

Take a moment to go outside or look out your window. Look at the trees, the sky, the birds, the road. Look toward the horizon. Look at everything around you. Soak it in. Appreciate it. Just stand quietly and absorb it for a moment.

Now, imagine that life has a voice, and imagine it's whispering in your ear while you look.

"Someday ... the sun will go out. Someday, what you are

looking at—every single solitary inch of it—will not be here. Every tree, every house, every building, every car, every road, every blade of grass, every insect, every dog, every human being … all of it will be gone.

"Every bird, every mailbox, every body of water, every animal. Everything before your eyes, behind you, under you. Gone.

"Every inch of everything that you can take in—all of it and what's beyond will be gone. The ground beneath your feet right now … gone. This was all part of the design from the moment of creation.

"Someday … the sun will go out."

Whether you believe in God, Allah, or some other Supreme Being, whether you believe there is an afterlife or you believe in none of it, one thing seems clear: the sun will go out, and Earth, one way or another, will be destroyed. Is this a horrible thing? Is this a tragic thing? No, it is simply a part of the process of life. The sun will not go out as a way to seek vengeance on us. The sun will go out because the sun is a star, and that's what stars do. Like any star, the sun will burn, live, and, by design, eventually burn out. And Earth will be destroyed. Human beings might escape Earth prior to its destruction or they might not. Regardless, this is of no matter to the sun.

The point here is simple: there is a reality that lies beyond the bounds of the way of life we've created. I wanted to shake up your relationship with the physical structures that fill up your senses. What does it take to imagine that everything—every inch of the physical reality that we experience as permanent—is gone? Yes, it likely won't happen for billions of years, but that is not what's significant. The significance of imagining the absence of all life as we know it is to simply bring present the paradigm *life*. There is a drama unfolding on this planet that is bigger than our way of life, and it is unfolding without regard to human beings, without regard to any species, and without meaning or judgment. There's no doubt that we are part of life, and that what we've created—our way of life—is part of life. That, though, isn't quite the way we've been taught to see it.

Questions for Further Discovery

1. Were you able to imagine that everything was gone? How did that make you feel?

2. What did the exercise in this chapter teach you about your relationship to physical structure? What was it like to experience the absence of everything?

3. You experienced that absence of everything in your mind. Ever wonder why it's all there in your mind to begin with? Do you see any connections to that and how you live?

CHAPTER 7

"The Curtain, Please!"

I once had a friend who originally was from Germany. He lived in the United States for many years, and by the time I met him, he had learned to speak English fluently. He told me that when he first came to America, he struggled to learn the English language. Time passed, but he made very little progress.

Finally, someone took him aside and spoke to him in German. "Stop thinking in German. Stop thinking in German and trying to translate it into English. *Think in English.*"

My friend didn't know what to make of this. "Think in English? But I know very few words."

"Use the words you have, and put those words together. Think in English!"

At first, thinking in English was extremely difficult for him, and he didn't even really know what it meant—thinking in German was all he ever had known. But he practiced thinking in English, forcing himself to use the words he knew, and over time, thinking in English dramatically improved his capacity to learn the language.

Creating the new paradigm will be like learning a new language—or more appropriately, it will be like learning language all over again. As we've seen, our outer world was constructed with the very intricate yet simple process of design:

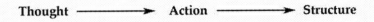

Thought ──────────▶ **Action** ──────────▶ **Structure**

This process led to all the physical structures we see when we look out into the world. This process also led to the mental structure that each one of us carries within us, a very dynamic system of thought—a paradigm—of how to live. Simply put, this process led to your mind – all the thoughts running through your head resulted from life in the current paradigm.

Additionally, our minds are intricately connected to our physical and emotional responses, and so we experience each moment of life holistically. Something happens in a moment, and your mind reacts with lightning speed, sending signals throughout your nervous system, which results in physical and emotional reactions. Those reactions are all learned responses. You've learned how joy feels and have connected the experience of joy with thoughts about joy, and you have connected the thoughts about joy to what is happening (events) in physical reality that caused the joy. You've learned how betrayal feels and have connected the experience of betrayal with thoughts about betrayal, and you have connected the thoughts about betrayal to what's happening (events) in physical reality that caused the feeling of betrayal. Your mind, body, and emotions represent a holistic system through which you experience life, moment by moment.

Now, imagine that you have your annual physical checkup, and your doctor discovers that you have cancer. Your doctor has to deliver a difficult prognosis. "I'm sorry," he tells you. "You probably only have four to six months to live."

Thoughts flood your mind: "What? How can this be? I feel fine. What am I going to do? *What am I going to do?* What about the kids and my spouse? This is going to devastate them. This can't be. It just *can't be.* We had so many things that we wanted to do. This can't be happening. It just can't. I'll never get to see my kids graduate. I'll never see them get married. I'll never see my grandchildren. What am I going to tell my parents? I don't want to die!"

Imagine the emotions you would experience once you realize that in six months or less, you will no longer be alive. Is your heart breaking? Imagine how that would feel in your body. Do you feel weak in the knees? How fast is your heart beating? Do you feel as if you might vomit?

You will never see your family or your friends again—the people you love most in your life. Imagine all the good times you've had with them. Imagine all that you had planned to do. *You're not going to do any of it.* You will be gone, and those people will have to live on without you. How will your children, your parents, and your spouse carry on without you? Feel the emotion. Feel this experience in your chest, in your gut.

Alternatively, you might imagine that it's not you who's going to die. Instead, it's your child, your spouse, or your parent—anyone you love deeply. See that person in your mind's eye, laughing, playing, and living ... and then gone.

Make sure that you've created a powerful experience in your mind, body and emotions of what the impending death—yours or another's—would be like. You would experience the impending death holistically. Hold on to that experience.

Now, imagine your doctor calls you a week later, apologizing profusely and explaining that there was a mistake in the lab. As it turns out, you do not have cancer. In fact, you are in perfect health. While you may be upset with your doctor, any anger over this mistake would take a backseat to the elation you would experience at learning you are not about to die. Your reality has shifted. The inaccurate conclusion—the thought that has been creating your experience—has been dispelled, and you are set free from the emotional roller coaster you've been riding.

The current paradigm has the same effect on us. We live day to day in an experience that is based on an inaccurate conclusion. Its impact is powerful, but nevertheless, the conclusion is inaccurate. Each day you walk around, as we all do, just living your life. You have thousands of thoughts per day that create your experience. Think about a moment in your life. Think about Monday morning. You are sound asleep, dreaming peacefully, when suddenly your alarm goes off, and you are awakened by its "BEEP! BEEP!" As you wake, there it is to greet you—your experience of life. Your mind fills with thoughts of the things you are facing this coming week, and this instantly fills you with an emotional and physical response. If you are one of the vast majority of people, your experience is, to some degree, on the downside of life, and you might think something like "Here we go again. It's time for the grind." For an instant, you may wonder how you are possibly going to do this same routine for the next twenty years, day after day, week after week, year after year. In a moment, you may see your entire life in front of you, and it all looks and feels the same. "What else is there?" you may think. You throw off the covers, and you sigh, "This is life," as your heart aches, and you start longing for the weekend. You think again, "This is life."

No, it isn't! This is not life! What you're experiencing is *not* life! What you're experiencing is *life in this design!*

I am the doctor, and I am here to tell you, "You don't have cancer." From the moment you were born, you began experiencing life. As you grew, you learned about life. You learned that there is war and poverty and cars and work and government and romance and family and school—all of it. You learned how you were supposed to feel about all these things. You were taught what was good and what was bad. You learned how you were supposed to live. The people around you didn't just teach you how to live; they taught you the right way to live. They taught you *the* way to live. You learned that you should feel good about certain things and feel bad about other things. You learned what trust and guilt and love and romance and relationships meant. You observed life, you participated in life, you experienced life, and from all that you drew conclusions about life and the world and what was possible in life. The only problem with all of it is that you weren't observing life. You weren't learning about life. You were observing and learning about life *in this one design.*

In the context of creating what you want—a new way of life—you must be clear what you are dealing with. With respect to our way of life, we created the structures, and we created the effects. We created the experience we live in each day. We also created the methods of dealing with the effects. From all of this, we created conclusions about what's possible in life. We created the beliefs of how people are supposed to live, and in doing so, we created every thought in our minds.

The only problem with all of it is we weren't drawing conclusions about life; we were drawing conclusions about life *in this design.* This doesn't mean we didn't learn anything about life itself, but we've made no distinction between life and life in this design. Creating a new way of life won't mean that people won't die—death is a part of life. It won't mean we won't have to work—making a living is a part of life. It does mean, though, that when you say or think things like "Poverty is a part of life," or "People are greedy," or "Life is hard," these may be inaccurate conclusions. We don't have a full set of data upon which to base those conclusions, so the best we can conclude is that poverty has resulted *from this design of life,* or that people's capacity for greed is accentuated *in this design of life,* or that our experience of life has been hard *in this design.*

This isn't about blaming "the system." The current paradigm is just something that has been designed, and its design produces particular results. This is about the decisions we've made about life, people, the world, and how to live, based on our experience of living in what we've already created. The current paradigm doesn't justify anyone's actions. It doesn't justify stealing, murdering, or going to a job you hate, but the blaming, the finger pointing, the justification—that all occurs inside the current paradigm. It's easy for the law-abiding citizen to demand accountability from the criminal. If I attempt to demand accountability from you, however, you likely would become defensive. If I said to you, "Look, you're making choices every day regarding your life," you likely would acknowledge it as a choice—but the choice of what? The choice between working at a job that's unsatisfying or living on the streets? The choice between feeling the pressure of making the mortgage or resorting to a life of crime? The choice between providing for your children or running off to Maui to escape your responsibility? Whenever you are feeling stressed, upset, depressed, or as if you have no choice but the lesser of two evils, you are fully experiencing the impact of the current paradigm and the limitation of your thought. You are experiencing the impact of the current paradigm, and it doesn't feel like you have any choice in the matter of your life.

The choices I'm talking about only give you more of what you want. Stop and contemplate this once more: *The choices I'm talking about only give you more of what you want.* Let that sink in. The new paradigm is not obvious, nor is it to be found in what we've already created. The new paradigm is not an improved current paradigm; it is a distinct way of life.

Pretend that you could go back to the moment when human beings first appeared on the planet and have a look around. There were no buildings, skyscrapers, roads, cars, or telephone lines. There were no airplanes, houses, or power plants. There was just what life had created. On the "canvas" of life, humans began to engage in the process of design—choice/chance and effect. We whirled our way through time. We zigged and then we zagged. None of this was necessarily done with any consciousness to move toward any destination. It was just people living and designing. The current paradigm was not planned in a boardroom. It was a chaotic process that somehow, in some way, caused us to end up where we are today—at this one particular destination, this one possible way of life.

Now, stop the action and hit the rewind button in your mind, and move back in time again to the appearance of humans. Here we are again—humans appeared on the planet to find only the "canvas" that life had made before them. Again, move forward in your mind, but now imagine that our ancestors made significantly different choices in how people should live. We zagged and then zigged. We whirled our way differently through time, but for some reason—it could have been because of chance, or it could have been because of choice—we ended up at an entirely different destination than what we are experiencing today. We arrived at entirely different conclusions about life, about how to live, and about what's possible in life.

Clearly, we cannot go back in time and make different choices, but it's not necessary that we do so. Right or wrong, good or bad, we ended up at the destination we did; there's no disputing that. The current paradigm is not wrong; it's just what we created, and it resulted in physical structure as well as a world of thought and decisions that we've made about what we created. The fundamental questions, then, are simply whether what we've created is giving us what we want, and if it's not, then how do we create what we want?

When we think about things, we expect them to be innovated. And yes, on some level, we expect our way of life to evolve. But think about this: when you think about the future of human beings on this planet—our evolution—does it include walking away from the pursuit of technology? Does our evolution include returning to hunting and gathering? Does it include leaving business behind us? What about religion or government? I'm not suggesting our evolution should or shouldn't include any of these things. It's important to be able to see the new paradigm as a separate and distinct thing from the current paradigm. You cannot create anything new unless you can see what you are creating as distinct from what you already have created.

Some believe that we are living at the cusp of a spiritual awakening. The implication seems to be that something is going to happen, and an immense goodness is going to be released on this planet, after which we will all learn to get along. While I am not against this type of awakening, I believe that, instead, we are going to experience a consciousness of choice. I believe our awakening will simply be that we are the first generation that is conscious of the fact that we can design a way of life. Creating the new paradigm is not the "pathway." In fact, it's not a pathway at all; it's a destination.

To suggest that the new paradigm is a pathway would be like thinking of the *current paradigm* as a pathway. It would be like thinking of a car as a pathway. The current paradigm is not a pathway—it's not a philosophy, method, or religion. The current paradigm is filled with these things, but it is not these things, and neither is the new paradigm. They're both destinations.

Are you beginning to see the possibility of a new destination, a new way of life, a … new paradigm? And if so, what do you see? What is the new paradigm?

Questions for Further Discovery

1. Can you see that where we are today is just one possible destination? How does the idea that what you're experiencing is "life in this design" versus "life" alter your relationship to what you're experiencing?

2. What are some fundamental decisions you've made about life, people, and the world? How do these decisions impact the way you live?

CHAPTER 8

The New Paradigm

Remember the description of our way of life given in chapter one? We're born, grow up, go to school—the standard progression with which we're all familiar. If this is our way of life, though, where do we begin to design a new way of life? Do we change business? Do we go back to farming, or hunting and gathering? Where do we look to find this new way of life?

If it seems difficult to see, you may be operating under the assumption that *all of the possible ways to live have already been invented.* The answer will not be found in our current way of life. The answer lies beyond business, beyond farming, beyond all of it. We are designing a new way of life, not another way to do business.

We got where we are today by asking questions such as "How do we design farming? How do we design the car? How do we design the computer? How do we design government? How do we design business?" We did not get our way of life by designing a way of life; we got our *way of life* by designing individual structures. We designed individual structures, and a holistic structure (a way of life) resulted. When the car was invented, it began with people being creative with the knowledge they had—and then the idea of the car took hold, and it shaped our way of life.

And so if we want to design a way of life, the question becomes "How do we design a way of life so that _____?" So that … what? In what way do we want to design this way of life? How is our way of life currently designed? Again, if designing individual structures resulted in a way of life, then it begs the question: "What is the way of life that resulted?" The description of our way of life from chapter one tells us what we do, but it doesn't tell us the *way life is for us*. We go to school, and we work for thirty to forty years of our life, but why do we do all these things? We do all these things to live—to buy a car, to buy a house, to eat, to go on vacation, to have money so that we can socialize and spend time with our family and friends, to provide for our families. We work at our jobs so that we can live, so that we can have the good things of life—and that doesn't simply mean physical things. Being happy is a good thing of life. Being satisfied is a good thing, too. We work hard so that we can have good things. "It don't come easy," as Ringo Starr sings. So we designed individual structures, and this resulted in a way of life, and that way of life dictates that we work hard to have good things. Good things come into our life from working hard (i.e., good things don't come into our life easily). Good things don't come into our lives naturally.

> **Principle of the New Paradigm: In the new paradigm, our way of life is designed so good things happen naturally for people.**

Can you even imagine what it would be like to live in a way of life where good things happen naturally for people? And how do we design a way of life where good things happen naturally? The moment we ask a question like this, what often arises are more questions, "Well, what about _____?" So we think, "What about eating? We have to eat." There is no denying that the physical universe imposes some restrictions on us, but the physical universe also imposed the restriction of gravity on us, and still we were able to create a way to fly that obeyed the laws of gravity and aerodynamics. Any way of life that we create will have to obey the laws of the universe. We also will have to design a way of life that meets our needs. We must eat, drink, sleep, and have shelter, but after that, anything goes—we are free to invent anything, including how we're going to get those basic needs met.

"But what about what's already here? We are already committed to a way of life. What should we do? Are you suggesting we just destroy it all?" Of course not. Did we destroy record albums when we created cassette tapes? Did we destroy cassette tapes when we created CDs? Did we destroy CDs when we created MP3 players? No, we simply created. Was the effect of creating cassette tapes that record albums were phased out? Absolutely. Was the effect of creating CDs that cassette tapes were phased out? Of course. Will the effect of creating MP3 players be that CDs are phased out? That remains to be seen. One thing we know for sure is that CDs will be phased out if there is no longer a need for them. Similarly, did we destroy hunting and gathering in order to create farming? Did we destroy farming in order to create business? No, we just created. There is no doubt that hunting and gathering was impacted, even destroyed in most places, by the invention of farming, and farming was impacted by the invention of business, but still, it was the act of inventing that had the impact on the former way of life.

As we design the new paradigm, it's important to remember that whatever concerns we have today in the current paradigm may not be a concern in the new paradigm. Eating will always be a concern, but who will perform a particular job, for example, may not be a concern, because that job might not exist in the new paradigm.

If we really engage in designing a way of life where good things happen naturally for people, one possible effect is that some or all of the existing structures of our world, including business, might be phased out. Business won't be phased out because it collapses. It will be phased out because, like everything that is phased out when you create, there is no longer a

63

need for it. *It will be phased out because we designed a way of life where good things happen naturally for people, and business was not necessary for us to live.*

I don't know whether or not business will cease to exist; I cannot predict the future. I honestly don't have an intention toward business, one way or the other. Now, having said that, is it possible that business will one day collapse? Yes, it might, but it won't collapse because we're creating a new way of life. It will do so because – like my square-wheeled wagon – something about its design was defective in the first place.

You may wonder, then, why we don't just design *business* (instead of a way of life) so good things happen naturally for people? Designing a way of life doesn't mean we'll never design individual structures just like designing a car involved designing individual parts, but starting with this question assumes that business is necessary for people to live a way of life where good things happen naturally. What if, despite its benefits, working in business, which is only one outcome in one possible design of life, is fundamentally a limit to a way of life where good things happen naturally for people? Focusing on designing a way of life doesn't assume anything about business—it is not about business or getting rid of business; it's not about running water, or electricity, or anything else that we've already created. It's about designing a way of life where good things happen naturally for people, and whatever structures are necessary to support that way of life will emerge (or remain) as an outcome of design—and those that are no longer necessary will be phased out.

With respect to the current paradigm, everything that's been created was done to make life better for people. We've only missed the mark to the extent that what we've created doesn't give us what we want. Creating a new way of life allows us to get our collective eye back on the ball. It reminds us why we created it all in the first place and that what we created—whether it's business or the car or the computer or government or capitalism or money or something in our own life—was *not the point of creation*. The point of creation was to give us more of what we want. In the domain of design, the only relevant question, then, is "Does what we've created give us more of what we want?" If the answer is yes, that's great. If the answer is no, then all there is to do is to turn our attention away from what we've already created, and focus it on what we want to create.

You may be thinking that it sounds like utopia, but it's not— *it's design*. This does not mean that bad things will never happen. Read the design principle of the new paradigm closely. It states that in the new paradigm, our way of life will be designed so that good things happen naturally for people. Its focus is on how good things will come into our lives, naturally (by design), instead of through a lot of hard work (by design).

With our destination clearly defined—a way of life designed so good things happen naturally for people—the question remains, "How do we go about designing this way of life?"

The answer to that question is simple: You already know how.

QUESTIONS FOR FURTHER DISCOVERY

1. Have all the possible ways to live already been invented? What do you think?

2. Imagine a way of life where business (or government or politics or technology) is not necessary for us to live. Don't get caught up in how that might occur; just imagine what it would be like. Can you do it?

3. In your own words, what does a way of life where good things happen naturally for people look like?

CHAPTER 9

Not of This World

If you're like most people, you probably have opinions about your effectiveness in life. You may have some thoughts—or even doubts—about your ability to create. I want to put any negative thoughts to rest right now.

Your ability to create—to have the things you want in your life, to create a new way of life where good things happen naturally for people—is not the issue.

Let me say it again: *Your ability to create is not the issue.*

Of course, I don't know your experience. I don't know how your parents raised you or what traumas you've suffered in life. You might feel overwhelmed by the idea that you can create what you want. You might think, "I know, I know. I'm a capable adult who can create anything I want, and the only reason I don't is I'm not disciplined enough, or I don't have enough courage, or I don't have enough time or I don't _____." You can fill in the blank for yourself. What I'm getting at is that for most of us, based on where we are today and how we got here, we live, stuck with some reason for why our ability to create what we want has been compromised.

Still, your ability to create is not compromised. Did you need to be taught how to draw the line from A to B in the exercise at the beginning of this book? No, I gave you an instruction, and you put the content of my instruction into the creative process.

Thought 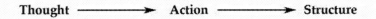 **Action** ———————➤ **Structure**

You thought about drawing the line for a split-second, and then you acted upon that thought, which resulted in you drawing in a line from A to B. The only thing impacting the result was the paradigm that influenced your design choice. You could have asked, "How do you want the line drawn? Do you want a straight line, curved line, or three-dimensional line?"

You might protest, "But drawing a simple straight line isn't the same thing as creating a way of life or a better job or making more money?"

Perhaps.

Clearly, there are some significant differences between drawing a straight line on a piece of paper and inventing a new way to live (or finding a better job, making more money, etc.). In the normal course of events, any rational person would dismiss the comparison as ridiculous—that's predictable and reasonable, but such a dismissal lacks critical thinking. It ignores the question "How are these things the same?" From a design perspective, all of these things, including the objection that they are different, are content added to the *mechanism*—the process of creation.

Your design problem is not that you cannot create what you want. Your primary design problem is that you *continue to create what you don't want*. You are an expert at creating; you create every moment of every day. You cannot not create. Your life did not result from what you didn't create; your life resulted from what you created. Creation is an affirmative act. So your greatest challenge is not learning to create; your greatest challenge is to stop creating that which no longer serves you. The reason this seems so difficult is simply because no one ever taught us to recognize the difference.

We all try to live a good life. We try to make sound choices that will lead to happiness, so it may be hard to comprehend that the answer is "Just focus on what you want, and stop focusing on what you don't want." We all face difficulties in life—perhaps you hate your job or you're unhappy in your marriage. Maybe good things are not happening in those places, naturally or otherwise, but it's unrealistic for you to just walk away. Questions that arise over life's difficulties usually do not have simple black-or-white answers. The key, though, is *those questions don't have anything to do with creating the new paradigm.* This is not about fixing the problems in your life that resulted from life in the current paradigm. This is about creating a new way of life for all people on this planet.

And so, designing a way of life so good things happen naturally for people is designing a way of life so good things happen naturally for people. Yes, you read that correctly: *designing a way of life so good things happen naturally for people is designing a way of life so good things happen naturally for people.*

It is *not* finding fulfilling work, it's *not* finding a spouse, it's *not* following your dreams, it's *not* building strong relationships, and it's *not* making a lot of money. It's not quitting your job or risking it all to follow your passion. It's also not staying at your job, and it's also not that you won't have to work. It's not renouncing your possessions, and it's not leaving your family and running off to Maui to live on the beach. It's not making less money, and it's not spending the rest of your life with your current spouse if you are dissatisfied with the relationship (nor is it leaving your spouse because you are dissatisfied with the relationship). It's not living a risk-free life and avoiding all challenges, nor is it living unattached.

It's also not that you won't end up with fulfilling work, or being happily married, or making a lot of money, or quitting your job, or renouncing all of your possessions. It's not that you won't end up with any of these things or at any of the particular destinations you currently desire. In fact, if a way of life where good things happen naturally for people is to be equated with anything, it's a way of life filled with the things people want.

I'm not telling you to think positively about what you've already created—that is, if you are unhappy in your marriage, you should walk around mindlessly chanting, "My marriage is great. My marriage is great." Instead, I'm actually trying to shift your attention away from what you've already created and from saying anything about it at all. I want you to understand the difference between what you already have created and what you're now creating. I want you to see that what you've already created—other than it being a guide to what you want to create—*has absolutely nothing to do with creating what you want.*

What we've created is real. It's all real. People really do have to get up to go to work. Some people live in poverty and others are rich. Some people live tremendously great lives, while others are miserable. Still, this isn't about fixing what we've already created. It's not about doing anything with what we already created. And no, this doesn't mean we should ignore the starving, the poor, or those less fortunate. That's really the point – putting your focus on what's already here as access to creating what you want is a distinct act from creating what you want. One is not the same as the other, but we live like they're the same.

Wherever you find yourself in life—right now, in this moment—you are experiencing life in the current paradigm. Your life is a holistic system wherein everything is connected. You want to make decisions to move your life forward, but each decision requires careful consideration of how it will impact the whole. Our way of life also is a holistic system wherein everything is connected. The same mind that created the conditions that led to the issues you're facing in your life also created the conditions that led to poverty, war, and hunger, and it's the same mind that reacts to and attempts to solve all these issues. The same fundamental system of thought you live your life with is the same system of thought that led someone in the world today to strap a bomb to his chest and blow himself up in the name of some god. It's the same mind that can't understand that focusing on what we want to create doesn't mean ignoring the less fortunate.

This is not about ignoring anything. The content of your life and the content of our way of life will be resolved as an outcome of designing a way of life where good things happen naturally for people. Remember, your design problem is not your ability to create; it's your inability to stop creating what you no longer want. And your life, our way of life didn't result from what we didn't create; it all resulted from what we created.

QUESTIONS FOR FURTHER DISCOVERY

1. Reflect deeply on the statement: "Your life did not result from what you didn't create; your life resulted from what you created." This statement is not as obvious as it seems. Consider that you actually live as if your life is a result of what you didn't create.

2. You operate with the same fundamental system of thought as someone who decides to strap a bomb to his chest and blow himself up in the name of some god. Think about the ways in which you and such a person are operating with the same fundamental system of thought. What do you see?

3. If I'm not saying to just ignore what we've created, what am I saying? Where should we put our focus?

CHAPTER 10

Meet Your Narrator

When I was a young boy, my father owned a pharmacy. There was no greater joy for me than to hang out with Dad while he worked. My "job" was to dust the shelves, and I loved it. Then one day, I had a thought: "Dusting the shelves is no fun. I don't want to do this anymore." But my parents, being good parents, tried to teach me responsibility, so regardless of how I felt about it, I continued to dust those shelves—and thus began my relationship with work.

As I grew older, I'd see people coming home from work and think that they didn't look very happy. When I'd hear people talk about work, they never seemed to have many positive things to say. I thought, "It seems odd that we spend so much time doing something we don't like." My work, of course, was school, and that didn't seem much better. I did well in school, but every week seemed the same. Of course, it was easy enough for me to assimilate the cultural thinking on work—"Monday morning blues," "Thank God it's Friday"—into my own thinking.

In college, I remember an ongoing joke with a friend. We'd see each other in the bathroom on Monday morning, when everyone was just dragging before going to class. I'd tell him, "It's really Friday."

"What?" he'd say.

"Well, you already woke up today, and that's the hardest

part, so today is already over, so it's Tuesday. Tuesday isn't so bad because by Tuesday, you're back into the flow of things, so it's really Wednesday. By Wednesday, you're already halfway home, and people are already beginning to talk about the weekend, so it's really Thursday. Thursdays are the best because the weekend is right in front of you. You can taste it. In fact, the party starts on Thursday night because who cares if we have to drag ourselves to class on Friday? It's only one day; anyone can do one day. So today is really Friday." We would go through this routine just about every Monday morning, coming up with different scenarios and explanations for why it was really Friday.

When I graduated college and started looking for a job, my resistance to work was strong, but then I had an epiphany. I knew the solution to my resistance to work: "I must find work of meaning. I must make a difference." So, I began my quest to find a way to cope with my resistance to work. Then, in 2002, I had an experience that cemented my ideas about work. I was visiting my parents. My father had sold his pharmacy in 1991 and was retired. We were sitting around the table after dinner when he said, "Man, I hate Sunday nights."

Puzzled, I asked, "Really, Dad? Why?"

He responded, "I still get that familiar feeling of having to go to work on Monday morning."

I couldn't believe it; I'd come full circle. My beliefs about work had been solidified. All the evidence was there.

Throughout this book, I've used the experience of work as an emotional trigger because it's been my issue. Hopefully, you can see this book is not about work. I could have referred to any aspect of our way of life and, by looking at it through the lens of design, brought you to the same place—we are living one possible way of life. Nevertheless, the focus of your life might not be work; in fact, you might not have a focus to your life at all. My sister, who grew up with the same parents working in the same pharmacy, has always loved work. So it's not who your parents are, and it's not your upbringing; it's not whatever issues, successes, and failures you've had in your life. It's just the impact the current paradigm has had on you. And your parents are the way they are because of the impact that life in the current paradigm has had on them. We've all been impacted in some way by this way of life.

My purpose in telling you this story was to introduce you to the part of me that narrates my life—my narrator. And I wanted to do that so you could be introduced to your own narrator.

From the time you were conscious of being alive, you began to notice things about life. One of the first things you may have noticed was that you had feet. Look at your feet right now. They belong to you. As far as you can remember, you never questioned that your feet were your feet. You never wondered whether your feet were your mother's feet, or your friend's feet, or the mailman's feet. No, they are your feet.

It's the same with your hands. Look at your hands. Those are your hands. At some point in time you became conscious of your hands and that they were your hands. They belonged to you. You never wondered whether your hands were your mother's hands, or your friend's hands, or the mailman's hands. It just wasn't something you thought about.

Another thing that's been around since early in life is your narrator. Who is this narrator? It's the voice in your head. Your narrator has been around since you can remember, describing life to you.

"Daddy's funny."

"I don't like dusting."

"She's cute."

"My mom looks so stressed from working."

"He never appreciates me."

"I must find work with meaning."

"If I'm being honest, I just don't love him anymore. I'm not sure that I ever really loved him."

"What can I expect? He's a teenager."

That's your narrator. Because it's always been with you, like your hands and your feet, you never questioned what the narrator was telling you.

Now, it might seem that it isn't a narrator at all; it's just you, thinking. But is it? Given what you now know about the current paradigm and that this isn't life but only life in this one design, which is filled with thoughts handed down from generation to generation, are you sure that the voice in your head—that which you consider to be you, thinking—isn't a voice reading from a script titled "Life in the Current Paradigm"? In other words, *are you sure the thoughts you've been having are really yours?*

Throughout this book, I've posed questions you might have, as if I knew what you were thinking. In doing so, I was voicing the thoughts of our collective narrator—the concerns and questions that I could anticipate from anyone living in the current paradigm in response to the ideas being presented.

The most impactful current paradigm thinking won't be found in highly intellectualized principles like the principles that make up business. The most impactful current paradigm thinking is found in our everyday conversation, our moment-to-moment reactions to life. It's found in those seemingly innocent thoughts that we may think are simply a description of what's happening in reality:

"I don't like shopping."

"I can't believe this traffic jam!"

"If you're going to be successful in business, you must have a website."

"How am I going to pay these bills?"

Your life is mostly lived by your narrator's watching what's happening in physical reality—like it's on a big movie screen—pulling lines from the script of the current paradigm and reading the script to you, which is followed by the crew (your body and emotions) reacting to the story.

The intention of examining life from the design perspective is so that you can create what you really want, and to that end, the script, which is filled with the decisions from experiencing life in this one design of life, doesn't always serve you. We need to more fully understand what the narrator is reacting to, and with that understanding, the narrator will become quiet, naturally. We need to answer the question: "When the narrator is chirping away, describing what's happening in physical reality, from a design perspective, what is it that the narrator is describing, commenting on, and/or reacting to?" In other words, the narrator responds to different things, people, and events that are happening, but collectively, from a design perspective, what do those things represent?

We'll explore the answer to this question in the next chapter.

QUESTIONS FOR FURTHER DISCOVERY

1. List different areas of your life or situations where you know the narrator is whispering in your ear. What seems to be the fundamental purpose of the narrator?

2. Have you had a focus to your life? Work? Relationships? If so, what is the dominant story that the narrator has told about the focus of your life?

3. What might being aware of the narrator make possible with regard to how you live your life?

CHAPTER 11

The Future

You might be thinking that in theory, all this talk about a new paradigm sounds great, that it would be great to live in a new way of life, but we simply don't. The reality is nothing is going to change tomorrow. You still have to go to work; you still need to make money. How does any of this make a difference in how we will live our lives today? It may sound easy, but "Dammit, life is just not that simple."

Life is not that simple? Or ... *life in this design* is not that simple?

"Call it what you want, but I have things to worry about and accomplish in the future. I have a life to live. I have responsibilities. Let's get back to reality."

Ok ... let's.

In reality, in physical real world, objective reality—*the future doesn't exist.*

There is *no* future in reality.

"Be present." "Live in the present." "Let the future emerge." You might be familiar with these slogans for how to live a better life. People long have talked about living in the present. "Letting the future emerge" or "emergent future" seem to be somewhat new concepts. But as New Age as living in the present and letting the future emerge may sound, it really isn't so new at all. It isn't New Age, because as far as we know, there isn't anything else possible. You can't do anything other than live in the present. You can't do anything *other than* let the future emerge. That's what's been happening; that's all that ever has happened. Can you live in the present moment and also live in another moment? Can you do something other than wait for the next moment to come? If you're impatient or upset because life isn't moving fast enough for you, can you do anything to make the future come faster? No, you can't. This moment is all there is, and then the next moment, and then the next moment, and so on.

We certainly can think about the future, talk about the future, and dream about the future.

But when you are talking about the future, when is it?

The present moment.

And when are the things you're talking about going to happen?

The present moment—a different present moment, for sure, but a present moment nonetheless.

And how will we get to that present moment?

The future will emerge.

Does the fact that there is no future in reality mean we can't impact the future? Absolutely not. All we are doing in each present moment is impacting the future. Even just sitting on a couch all day on Sunday, watching television, is having an impact on the future. Any choice or action in a present moment will have an impact on some present moment in the future. If I drop a letter in the mailbox in this present moment, I'm taking an action that will impact a present moment in the future—your receiving my letter.

So what's the big deal about the future?

The big deal is in looking at the future from the context of design. From the context of design, the future is nothing but a mental construct. It only exists in your mind, and there is nothing in the "future" but what you put there. The "future" is the place from which we create. It's the place from which the whole creative process of life is born. (Thought yields action yields structure.) So the challenges posed at the beginning of this chapter are legitimate. On one hand, it sounds great in theory, but how does it help us impact the future? How does it help us impact the future, especially when, predictably, next Monday, you probably will go to work at the same job? But you also could be dead next Monday—but that's really not the point, because whenever you reach next Monday, *it will still be the present.* And you know what you'll likely be doing next Monday morning, there in the present? *You'll be thinking about the future as if the future is real.* You might think, "Ugh, I can't believe I have to make it through another week." And in a flash, this will conjure up an emotional and physical experience consistent with that thought. In that moment, you'll have created your future, and it will grip you like a vice, keeping you locked in that experience. Instead of creating what you really want, you'll be living, just trying to survive what you've already created.

You don't even need to wait until next Monday to conjure up that experience in your mind. You can experience that future—waking up on Monday morning, thinking about the week ahead of you—right now in this present moment, just by thinking about it. Even though it isn't happening, you can evoke that thought and experience it, and that thought, like any other, will impact your actions *in this present moment.*

I'm not saying that what you need is positive thinking. What I'm telling you is there is no future in reality; the future only exists as a mental construct, and there's nothing in the future except what you put there. The very thought of using positive thinking—for example, manipulating your mind and walking around chanting, "Monday's are great" in order to feel better—is you, adding something to the future. If you do have that thought about what to do next Monday morning, then that's you, adding that thought to the future, and you're only adding that to the future as a response to *what's already in your future*—your opinion of Mondays.

You might argue, though, that the future certainly exists. Even if you drop dead two minutes from now, in five minutes, something is going to be happening somewhere.

When five minutes have passed, however, it will still be the present (and you won't care because you'll be dead). Still, it's true that something is going to happen five minutes from now. And that's really the point: something is going to happen, but what is that "something"? Just as in every present moment, that something that will happen is *an outcome of past design*.

Still, you might argue, you are going to work next week. Unless you die, you know you're going to work. You're not running off to Maui. You're not quitting. It's that simple. Maybe you're going to work because you must because of past design, but whatever the reason, the fact is you're going.

If there was ever a time to pay close attention, this is the time. What I'm going to tell you is not intuitive; it's not the way we've been conditioned to think about things, but if you can understand what I'm saying, it will change your life forever. In the last chapter, I posed a question about the narrator: When the narrator is chirping away, describing what's happening in physical reality, from a design perspective, what is it that the narrator is describing, commenting on, and/or reacting to? I'm trying to separate what's happening in physical reality from the creative process that begins with thought in our mind. What's happening in physical reality is *always the tail end of the creative process*. The moment you are experiencing right now is an outcome of past design. Each moment of life in physical reality is an outcome of past design, and each moment is *always the result of past thinking*.

This, though, is not the way we have been conditioned to think about it. Even with something as simple as meeting a friend for dinner next Thursday night. When you arrive at Thursday night, everything in physical reality is an outcome of past design. You made a decision at the beginning of the week to have dinner. The owner of the restaurant where you decided to have dinner chose to open the restaurant. Someone chose, at some time in the past, to construct the building where the restaurant is located. The chef chose to become a chef, and she chose to work at this restaurant. We decided, culturally, to have restaurants. We chose the medium of exchange: money. *What's happening in physical reality is always the outcome of past design.* We simply are not present to the massive design that went into creating this moment and—more important—that this moment is an outcome of past design. We don't live fully conscious that each moment of our experience is a by-product of past design. So whether you are observing a person, a place, a thing, or an event, whenever you put your focus in physical reality, what you are focusing on is always an outcome of past design. With respect to design, to creating what we want, we live our lives "head-deep" in outcomes of past design and call that reality. *And in truth, it is reality, but the fact that it is reality doesn't have anything to do with creating what you want.*

The content of your thinking today, *whatever it is,* will result in physical reality at some moment in the future, just as the content of yesterday's thinking (or last year's or last decade's or last century's thinking) has resulted in the physical reality that we are experiencing in this moment. Designing a way of life where good things happen naturally for people is *a future.* It's a destination, a vision. It's something that will exist in physical reality one day in the future, but it will only exist as a result of how we think between now and the moment of its existence.

So from a design perspective, what the narrator is responding to and interpreting is almost exclusively what exists today in physical reality. *The narrator is reacting to outcomes of past design, and it's only doing so because that's what it's been conditioned to do—to look out at physical reality to initiate the creative process.* The narrator is feeding you content based on what you've learned and observed living in this one design of life. We've been trained to believe that what's happening in physical reality has something to do with creating the future, and it doesn't. It simply doesn't (unless you say it does). We were never taught that what's happening out in physical reality is just an outcome of past thinking and action. And so if I say, "Create a new way of life," the narrator doesn't really stop to contemplate that question; instead, it looks out at the end-product of design—the physical reality—and reacts with "What about? What about the way of life that's already here? What are we going to do about that?" This thought becomes a concern that you put in the future to deal with as part of the process of design. *It becomes the future you are creating.*

If you were going to design a totally new car, would you need to do anything with the cars that are already here in physical reality? Likely, you wouldn't put your attention on what to do with the cars that already exist; instead, you'd focus on your picture, your vision of the car; some features you want the new car to have. You'd focus on designing your new car; you would just invent. Taking the outcome of past design of the millions of already existing cars and putting that outcome in your future, as something to deal with, just wouldn't make sense. Assuming that your car is objectively a better car, seeking to eradicate or fix all that's already been created would be a monumental task—nothing short of … "working hard to have good things." If you car is truly a better car, people will choose it, and the old car will be phased out naturally.

This example may seem ridiculous, but I promise you, *this is how you live your life.* You put your focus on what you've already created and the decisions and thoughts you have about it. You look out at physical reality to tell you what you can create and how you should create it. You evoke the mind of the current paradigm—all the decisions you've made about how to live and what's possible in life. You examine the action that you think it will take to achieve what you want, in order to help you decide whether the effort will be worth it. You try to decide whether you have enough time or discipline or knowledge. You put all of this in your future, most unconsciously, and then you attempt to create your life.

Your only issue of design is that you don't keep your focus on creating what it is that you want, and you don't stop creating what you don't want. And that's because you've never been taught to do so. You've been taught to focus on what's happening in physical reality and that what is happening there is key to creating what you want. But it isn't. *It's simply what we've created.*

You've been taught to focus your attention primarily on the action, the doing, as the key to creating what you want. Action is not the first step to creating what you want; *it's an outcome of thinking about what you want to create.* We have a tendency to see action as something separate from thought, rather than seeing action as the natural manifestation of thought. We even have sayings like "Action speaks louder than words" or "Just do it"—these show our reverence to action. In the realm of design, though, action never speaks louder than words. It can't. You may say something like, "It doesn't matter what I think. It doesn't matter how I feel. If I want to get something done, I'm just going to have to suck it up, push through, and do it." Then, you suck it up, push through, and accomplish what it is you set out to do. Guess what? The words you muttered and thought preceded those actions. You took action consistent with your thinking, and you likely experienced "sucking it up and pushing through." If, at some point, you think to yourself, "This grinding effort isn't working. I'm going to try another tack," those words will dictate your action. Your actions always flow naturally and effortlessly from your thoughts. Thought always precedes action, and there is no action without thought, just as there is no structure without action.

You must learn to keep your focus on creating what you want, and let the creative process, which starts with thinking and moves through action into physical structure, take over. It will. It always does. It's how you brought everything you already have into your life. It only ever seemed hard because you were simultaneously focused on and creating what you didn't want, and over time, it got so hard that you gave up creating what you really wanted, which only made life more of a struggle.

But what about the things our way of life requires of you today? Can you just ignore them?

No, do them—just don't confuse them with creating the new paradigm. You can participate in the life we created and create what's next. In fact, for the first time, you finally may be able to authentically live. You don't have to fake it anymore. You don't have to think positively about your life or fool yourself into thinking that it's what you really want. You can let go of the mental gymnastics and coping mechanisms that you use to survive the current paradigm. Your eyes are open, and you can see the life you've created for what it truly is—a mere outcome of design that began as thought and moved through action into physical reality. This is all to remind you that what we created isn't the point. The point of any creation is to give us more of what we want.

QUESTIONS FOR FURTHER DISCOVERY

1. Reflect on the fact that there is no future in reality. Describe the contents of the "future" that is already there for you, by default. Can you see that the content of your future is filled primarily with outcomes of past design?

2. Practice seeing what's happening in physical reality as an outcome of past design (i.e., the tail end of the creative process as distinct from the initiation of the creative process, which begins with the thoughts you are having right now). Where is your focus most of the time? Experience the connection that has been fused by conditioning between what's happening in physical reality and your thoughts. In your mind, can you find and experience the future that you want that is distinct from the past, from the outcomes of past design? This is often challenging for people so give yourself sometime to practice.

3. What things have you given up on? What story has the narrator been telling you about wanting and/or pursuing those things?

.

CHAPTER 12

A New Mind, A New World

Is this beginning to make sense? You may be thinking that this all seems great, but really, a lot of bad things happen in the world, and there is a lot to be done if we're going to create a new way of life, a new world. You even may ask, "Isn't there a danger that we'll end up with a lot of happy people living in the same world?"

Yes, that is a danger, if you put those concerns in your "future." If you take that thinking and place it into the creative process, if you reduce this to a technique to make you feel better about life in the current paradigm, if you dismiss this as a new philosophy or even a new slant on some old philosophies, then yes, we will end up with happy people walking around in the same world. Not everything I've written here is new thinking. What's key is the focus. This book is about designing a *new way of life*, and a way of life is more than just how you are feeling. A way of life is a holistic structure, and if the outcome is a way of life where good things happen naturally for people, and you are really engaged in designing that way of life, that's going to lead to a different world. On a global level, outcomes consistent with the current paradigm include the incidence of war, poverty, hunger, genocide, and so on. If these global issues continue to exist, it will be for one of two reasons: those things are a part of life, not life in a particular design; or, as hard as it may be to imagine (and as unlikely as it is), those things are somehow required for a way of life where good things happen naturally for people. And if they disappear, they'll do so naturally, as an outcome of designing a way of life where good things happen naturally for people.

So if you're thinking that all I've written is positive thinking, you haven't fully grasped the power of design. Designing a way of life where good things happen naturally for people absolutely includes feeling good and being happy and satisfied in life, but it also includes creating real, physical structures—macro structures that support people in having the things that we all need to live healthy, satisfying lives. In short, it includes whatever is necessary to live a way of life where good things happen naturally for people. As I've mentioned, this is not about creating utopia; it's about real people living real lives in a more fulfilling way.

To recap, life isn't just the way it is—it's all by design. Life itself is design. The evolutionary processes of life led to humans, not necessarily as an ultimate outcome but an outcome nonetheless. When we arrived on this planet, there were none of the man-made things we have today. There was only what life had designed. Humans, like every other living creature, began to engage in the process of design—chance/choice and effect. We designed and designed and designed. We created different ways of life, each with its own unique characteristics and consequences, both good and bad. Ultimately, we created our current way of life. At some point, we stopped and looked at the world we created. We saw (and, of course, still see) the masses starving and living in poverty. We saw war and violence, suicide and crime. We saw people working really hard to create a better life. We saw lots and lots of action. We saw all these things and more, and we made decisions about the world. We didn't relate to these decisions as decisions that we had made about what we had created; instead, these were decisions about the world, about life, about the way life works, and about people—even about human nature. We said things like, "The world is _____ (a cold place, scary)" or "Life is _____ (hard, unfair)" or "People are _____ (selfish, violent)." And in response to these decisions, we made decisions about how to live and what's possible in life.

It simply never occurred to us that what we were witnessing and what we continue to witness is a result of what we had created. Does this mean we haven't learned anything about life? No. Does it mean we didn't learn anything about people? Of course not. We've learned a tremendous amount about people. People certainly are hard-wired with the capacity for violence as well as for love. People have the capacity to kill with malice and then have lunch without giving their actions a second thought. Still, we began to hand down the decisions we made from generation to generation. There wasn't "Life in this design" versus "Life." It was all just life. It was "just the way it is." Now, of course, we are conscious that we made all this, but how about this level of consciousness—the moment. *The moment you are experiencing right now is by design.*

By the time you and I were born, there was the "world" out there, and we were just expected to learn how to live in it. No one ever said to us, "This is just one way to live—all that you see. Don't worry about it. It's all just the outcomes of design. It's just one result, and you're not stuck with any of it." It's likely that no one ever taught you that life is about creating. In fact, creating is all there is in life. You're never *not* creating, and if what's here isn't what you want, don't give your attention to it, because it's just an outcome of design. Instead, put your focus on what it is that you *do* want. Focus your attention there. That's the best way to create.

Before reading this book, you likely related to the world in the following way:

There is one world in physical reality.

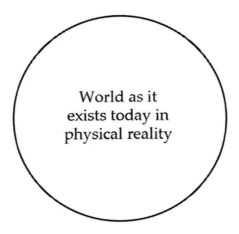

One world in physical reality

There is one world in your mind.

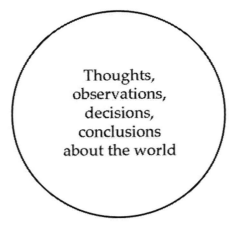

One world in your mind

You haven't necessarily consciously thought, "There's one world in my mind." It's just been "the world," and then the thoughts you've had about "the world."

One thing I will continue to emphasize is that the world today is a particular way. What we've created—the good and the bad—is real. Just like the cars we've created are real. Those decisions you've made about life, the fundamental beliefs you hold (whatever they are), are based on real-life experiences. With respect to design, though, *the subjectivity or objectivity of your experience in the current paradigm is irrelevant.* The question will always be: "That's what you've experienced. That's the world that you know; that's what's here; that's only where you've been taught to put your focus, but what is the world you're going to create?" So if you think I'm telling you to focus your attention on what's here and think, "The world is a great place," like some affirmation or as an act of denial, you are missing the point. I'm challenging you to *create a world that is a great place,* and how you create a world that's a great place is the way that you create anything. You create a new car by focusing on and creating it first in your mind. You create a new computer or relationship by focusing on and creating it first in your mind. You turn your attention, your focus, to that which you wish to create, while also understanding that while you are creating what you want, you are going to continue to live with what's already been created.

Before you read this book, you had a particular connection (albeit unconscious) between your thoughts and the world; I have been reconfiguring the connection between your thoughts and the world. In the realm of design, having the relationship with the world you've had would be like wanting to create a new car, when all your energy, creativity, and focus was on the car that already exists—all you talk about and think about is the old design. Certainly, you'd have to talk about the old design to the extent that you wanted to see it as distinct from the new car. In creating your life, however, there is no such conscious distinction. We speak of "the world," rather than being aware that we're speaking about "the world that resulted in this design."

And so, to design a new way of life—a new world—you need to understand that in physical reality, there is still (and always will be) just one physical world.

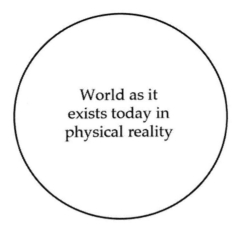

World as it
exists today in
physical reality

One world in physical reality

In your mind, though, with respect to creating, there must now be two.

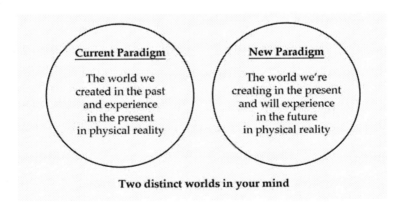

Current Paradigm

The world we
created in the past
and experience
in the present
in physical reality

New Paradigm

The world we're
creating in the present
and will experience
in the future
in physical reality

Two distinct worlds in your mind

The current paradigm is the world we created, and it exists in physical reality; the new paradigm is the world, the way of life we're creating. Does thinking about it this way mean that the current paradigm won't continue in physical reality? No, the current paradigm most certainly will live on. It will live on just as CDs continue to live on even though there are now MP3 players, or just as the old design of a car will continue on after there are new cars. Each of these things will continue, until there is no longer a need for it and it is phased out naturally. But now we know, the current paradigm is just an outcome of design

It's critical to understand the distinction between what's happening in physical reality and what's happening in your mind. It's the misunderstanding of this aspect of creation that prevents people from powerfully creating. They may scoff, "So, I'm just to imagine a fantasy world in my head, and it will magically appear? Yeah right." No, it won't appear magically, any more than a newly designed car would just appear magically. Change will occur in the only place it can—in physical reality through action. The action, though, won't be borne of the world we have created. It won't arise as a reaction to or be limited by the current paradigm. It will be borne of the world we are creating. In order for the change we want to result—that is, the new paradigm—we must imagine the world we wish to create as distinct from the world we've already created. We must break the grip of ingrained assumptions that tie our past to our future. This is how it works with anything we create. Yes, a new car will result in physical reality through action, but what action would you take toward building it if you had no picture in your mind of a new car that's distinct from the current car? People dismiss the value of imagining a new world as mere fantasy because it doesn't appear magically in an instant in physical reality. The world you want to live in, though, will never occur except by chance—unless you begin to see that world in your mind as a distinct thing from the world we've already created.

Ultimately, there may be consequences in physical reality—both good and bad—as a result of the world we've already created. In fact, fear of the negative consequences is what creates such a pull to keep dealing with the world that we've created. Some think the world is in crisis. They may say, "This is serious business. No time for this dilly-dallying. This is reality." The flaw in that thinking is that it equates creating a new world in

95

our minds with ultimately ignoring what's out here in physical reality. I tell you this: *You will live more in the present moment dealing with life in front of you by creating the world you want in your mind than you ever have by focusing your attention on the world we've created.*

Creating the new paradigm doesn't require us to believe that human beings are blank slates. It doesn't require us to believe that anything is possible. Before I fully understood the distinctions of design, I really struggled with certain things. Sometimes I'd think, "I could be in the wrong place at the wrong time and find myself the victim of a crime or act of violence. How do I reconcile that with creating the new paradigm?" And more important, I wondered whether I should just ignore the possibility that something like that might happen to me. In the end, though, whatever happens to us, creating is all there is to do. There isn't anything else. So when I walk down a dark street at night, I am cautious. I still have life insurance to protect my wife in case I pass away unexpectedly. And yes, I pay my taxes. The need for these things may certainly get phased out as a result of designing the new paradigm, but for now, I don't deny what's here.

When I do these things, which the current way of life requires me to do—for example, when I walk down a dark street with my hand on my wallet—I simply don't give it a lot of creative energy. I recognize that for whatever reason—systemic or not—someone could jump out from behind a building, point a gun at me, and demand my wallet. And if that ever happened, in that moment I would not care whether the person was stealing from me because of the current paradigm, or as a result of a systemic outcome, or because he was a mean, miserable human being. In that moment, I would likely care about one thing—living. I wouldn't care about why it was happening any more than a starving person would care why he has no food or any more than a person who loses his job cares why he was fired. Freedom comes from the realization that you're not stuck with what's here; what is here is just an outcome of design, and you can, if you choose, create something else.

I don't want you to learn to live in the present moment as a statement that the world is okay as it is. I'm not okay that people are starving. I'm not okay that people are living in poverty. I'm not okay with the suffering—whether physical or psychological—that people experience in this world. But I can let it be because I can see it for what it is—one outcome that resulted from past thinking, past design. And the fact that it's all in front of me in physical reality is irrelevant to my ability to create something else. It's all just one physical reality that resulted from design.

And so, you must begin to see the world with distinction. You must shift from witnessing one world in physical reality and relating to it as if it's "the" world, you must shift to witnessing what's happening in physical reality in context, as the world we've created so that in your mind, you can step out of what we've created and shift your focus to another thing—*the world we are creating*, the new paradigm.

In the realm of design, there is no black or white, right or wrong. There is only what you've created and what you're creating. I'm not suggesting that anything is possible, but you know what? Whether anything is possible is irrelevant. It certainly doesn't justify not creating what you want. Really, what choice do you have? If you live and breathe, you create. You're always creating something. Plus, anything doesn't have to be possible for all of us to live fulfilling lives. In the realm of design, you can be both a realist and a dreamer, both a critical thinker and a free spirit. In the realm of design, you don't have to be a blank slate in order to create what it is that you want, nor do you have to be limited by what's already been created. You don't have to live with the definitions you've been given. You can live in the world we've created with your eyes fully open, denying nothing, seeing it all for what it is—and if it isn't what you want, then, at the same time, you can create the world in which you want to live.

QUESTIONS FOR FURTHER DISCOVERY

1. Describe in detail the world we've created. Don't resist describing anything. Remember, it's just the world we've created—the good and the bad.

2. What are some decisions you've made about the world we've created? How do those decision impact how you live?

3. Describe the world you wish to create. Don't resist describing it because you don't know how to create it or it seems too difficult. Remember, creation begins with thought, and we can't create anything until we describe it in language.

4. You can live in this world without denying any of it, while creating the next. What do you think? Reflect on how you'll have to think differently (e.g., you'll have to keep what's happening in physical reality and how you react to it separate and distinct from the world you are creating). You'll have to see one thing as distinct from the other. How else will you have to think differently?

CHAPTER 13

The Edge of Language

Have you ever known someone who just amazed you? That person may seem impervious to life. He or she moves through life effortlessly, as if the rules of life don't apply. You may have said, "He has his own set of rules" or "She lives in a different world than the rest of us, a world all her own." This is the way you must begin to relate to creating the new paradigm—you must live in a different world, not the world you've inherited but a world all your own.

I've spent this entire book getting you to a place where you can begin to create the new paradigm. To do so, you must be able to hold two seemingly contrary thoughts in your mind: First, the world as it exists today *is* the world as it is exists today. It's not going anywhere just because we start thinking differently. Second, we are going to create the new paradigm right smack in the middle of this same physical reality that already exists. If we are successful in our creation, the new paradigm will exist in physical reality someday in the future, and the way in which we are going to bring that physical reality into existence is, first and foremost, by how we think between now and its existence.

The question, of course, is "How, in the midst of the world that we've already created, in the midst of all this physical structure, do we think so that the new paradigm—a way of life where good things happen naturally for people—comes into existence in physical reality in the future?"

On one level, depending on your knowledge and interest, it may seem like it's out of your hands; that it will take experts in many different fields to invent the new paradigm for you—economists, scientists, engineers, and other experts who will come up with new models and ideas that will help create a way of life where good things happen naturally for people. While there is no denying the impact of experts in shaping how we live, you don't need to wait for the experts to figure it out for you. The current paradigm didn't result because a handful of individuals created a new idea; ultimately, it resulted because of the way in which people chose to live. The new paradigm will result in the same way—from the way we each choose to live our lives.

To create the new paradigm, the question becomes "How would you live in a way of life where good things happen naturally for people?" Usually, when someone asks us to imagine the future, we imagine the physical structure we want—the circumstances we wish to experience. It might include dreams of living on a beach or having lots of money. The physical structure—your circumstances, the *good things* you want—will be part of what there is to create. You are, though, inventing a way of life where good things *happen naturally* for people, and so you'll have to go deeper and create a more holistic picture. You have to think about the purpose that physical structure serves in our lives. For example, what purpose does money serve? What purpose does a car serve? What purpose does a house on the beach serve? What purpose do all the things we've created serve? Structure allows us to live a particular way. What we are creating is a way of life where good things happen naturally for people, and that structure (like any other structure), whatever it ultimately will look like, will allow people to live a particular way. *It will allow you to live a particular way,* and so, what there is for you to do is to invent how you would live—in a way of life where good things happen naturally. You have to imagine yourself living in that reality and imagine how you would be living.

The thing to remember is that part of creating is distinguishing one thing from another. If we invent a new car, we keep distinguishing our new car from the old car. That's how we know we are creating a new car. When we invent a new way of life, we must learn to distinguish the old way of life from the new way of life. Today, you obviously know how life is for you. You live with the impact that life in the current paradigm has had on you. You know what it means for *you* to live in a way of life where people work hard to have good things. More importantly, you know what it means to *think* in a way of life where people work hard to have good things. There are beliefs that you have about yourself, the world, how to live, and what's possible in life.

You want to understand what those beliefs are and how they shape how you live. Step back and examine your life to date, as if you were studying the life of another, and ask yourself questions like, "What are the fundamental beliefs of the person living this life?"; "Does this person believe he can have what he wants in life?"; "How does this person pursue the things in life that are important to her?" Don't ask these questions to be judgmental; ask as an opportunity to understand the impact that the current paradigm has had on you. The current paradigm has shaped you in ways that are not apparent. Asking these questions allows you to begin to see who you've become as a by-product of living in this way of life, and to create an opening to invent who you are to become.

So perhaps you discover that you've lived as someone who doesn't really believe he can have what he wants—that's the impact that the current paradigm has had on you, and you think that in a way of life where good things happen naturally for people, people would fundamentally believe they can have what they want. This insight creates the opportunity to invent living as someone who can have what he or she wants. How would that person live? How would that person engage in each moment of life, each interaction?

Invent … and then start to live that way.

Or you may discover that you've lived as someone who

believes there aren't enough good things in life to go around. In the new paradigm, there will be enough for all. How would you approach life, living with an expectation that there is enough for all of us? How would this insight shift your thinking and how you see the world?

Invent … and then start to live that way.

Now, you may think that you can't always have what you want, and there isn't always enough for people. This is where you need to stay clear with your thoughts. That statement is absolutely valid and accurate. The question, though, is "Which world is that statement describing?"

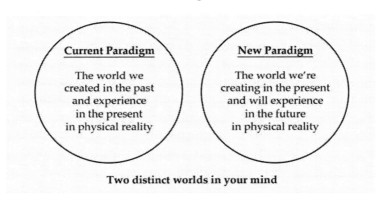

Current Paradigm

The world we
created in the past
and experience
in the present
in physical reality

New Paradigm

The world we're
creating in the present
and will experience
in the future
in physical reality

Two distinct worlds in your mind

Many would agree that it describes the world we've created, but do you want that to be the world we're creating? Certainly, even in the world we are creating you might not get what you want all the time, and sometimes there may not be enough. The intention here is for you to realize who you are in your life and how you live. A person who lives as if he can have what he wants may not always get what he wants, but he lives differently than a person who fundamentally believes he cannot have what he wants in life. A person who lives as if she can have what she wants *thinks* in a particular way, and therefore, she will *act* in a particular way and, ultimately, *live in a particular way.*

Who would you be in the living of your life?

How would you think?

How would you pursue the things that are important to you?

Who would you be in your relationships?

Who would you be in the living of your life?

There are no right answers to these questions. It's an invention.

Questions like these are meant to evoke the creative process. You recognize that the world before your eyes in physical reality is just one outcome. You are saying, "I will not evoke the system of thought that created all of this. I am creating the space to allow a new system of thought—a new mind—to emerge, and I'm doing that because that's how design works." You initiate creation, whether it's a car, a computer, an airplane, or a world, by giving it language.

Since we arrived on this planet, we've been seeking ways to live in the world. Like my fictitious Neo, we have sought to understand the world as it is, and each level of understanding impacted how we live. The one thing we weren't fully conscious of was that at some point in understanding the world as it is and finding ways to live in it, the world we were experiencing was no longer the world as it is. What we created came full circle and began to impact the world as it is. In short, we skewed the data without realizing we skewed the data. The ironic twist, then, is that to fully understand the world as it is, we had to learn that we participate in the creation of the world we experience; that we are always "catching up" to the world we created in thought.

I wrote this book to instill in you a desire for discovery. I want you to experience the power of design and all that design makes possible. I created a new vision that I hope will engage your imagination and pull you forth to seek new ways to make the new paradigm live in physical reality. And ultimately, that's really the point. This isn't a magical philosophy that will allow you to sit on the couch while life happens to you. *It's so much better than that.* It's regaining what truly has been lost to us—the experience of powerfully and fully participating in our lives. To wake up in a world where we get to act in ways that enliven us; to think in ways that bring our spirits alive—that's what's available. To experience the joy of action, rather than the burden of it—that's what's really possible. If life was meant for anything, it was meant to be lived. I've taught you how to think but only so that you can act—and act joyously.

And so today, the new paradigm might not live anywhere else in the world, but it must live in you. This is how design works. When Edison was working on the light bulb, it didn't exist in the world. The only place it existed was in him. When Mozart was composing *A Little Night Music*, it existed in him and for him before it existed for the world to share. I want to remind you that you are part of the world. Because we experience life by witnessing the world before our eyes, we don't experience ourselves as part of it. This is why when most of us hear our voice on tape or see ourselves on video, we are surprised by what we hear and see. "That's really me? That's really how I occur in the world?" we exclaim. We forget that for others, we are part of their world. To make the new paradigm live in the moment for you is to make it live in the world for others; *it's to make it live in the world.*

And when you do this, you will actually become evidence that the new paradigm is possible.

And just remember: don't beat yourself up trying to get somewhere. Begin where you are, and don't underestimate the power of where we've come. Before you read this book, there probably wasn't even the possibility of another world to create. There was no choice because no one taught you to invent the choices. Yes, this book has been about creating a new vision for human beings. That vision, though, isn't just about our future; it includes our vision of what's already here. By transforming our vision, our understanding, of what's already here, we've created the possibility of thinking and speaking powerfully about the future and the world we wish to create.

Ultimately, if what I've written here doesn't resonate with you in some (or any) way, let *it* be. It's just my self-expression, my point of view, and most importantly, remember, this book too is just an outcome of past design. Let it be and go find the voice that resonates with you, or create your own. For me, that act would be a demonstration of creating a way of life designed so good things happen naturally for people.

So give yourself some room to explore. Remember, you've spent your entire life trying to figure out how to live in this world. Now, you can spend the rest of your life creating the world you want to live in.

QUESTIONS FOR FURTHER DISCOVERY

1. Reflect on the following: A person (could be male or female, but for purposes here will be male) has just come home from work. He had a great day and is excited about some upcoming projects. He is in the kitchen, preparing dinner for his family. He is so happy, he is actually whistling while he works. A family member is watching television in the next room, and our person can hear it, but his attention is mostly on how good he feels. Then, he hears a commercial asking for money to feed starving children. At first, everything is fine, but then he begins to have the following thoughts:

   > Oh, those poor, poor children. It's just a shame that we live in a world where people are starving. My life is so great right now. I'm so lucky. I feel so grateful, but those poor, poor children. Maybe I should give some money. I've wanted to do it for a long time. I wonder how much it is? That reminds me that I have to pay that bill for the repairs to the roof. Wow, that was a lot more than I expected. It really threw off our budget. Speaking of budgets, where am I going to get the money to donate to those poor children? I haven't got a dime to spare. Joey needs braces and then Julie is going off to college in a couple of years. My god, I haven't started really saving for her college education. How the hell are we going to pay for that? I hope she can get some student loans or something. Maybe she'll want to go to a state college. It'll be cheaper. I know she really wants to be an architect, and none of the state colleges offer that. Well, she'll just have to go where we can afford. I mean I know I got to go to a great school, but times are so different now. Oh, I'm a horrible parent. … Oh, those poor children. The world is such a harsh place. Life is so hard. Those poor, poor children.

   Can you relate to this person? What fundamental beliefs does this person hold about himself, life, and the world?

How do think those beliefs impact how he lives? Can you see how this person has reacted to physical reality and put things in his future? Can you see the entire process was occurring in his thinking? How do you think this person pursues the things that are important to him?

2. Write the story of your life to date. What does your story say about you, the person who is living it? What fundamental beliefs do you hold about yourself, life, people, and the world. How do those beliefs impact how you've lived?

3. Write the story of the life you'd live in a way of life where good things happen naturally for people. Who would you be in a way of life where good things happen naturally for people? How would you live?

CHAPTER 14

A Life Worth Living

Taken at face value, it may seem as if I'm expecting too much by questioning everything about your life, about life, for the hope of a new way of life.

But it's not hope; it's design.

It's just that we have lived so long with the belief that we won't do good things for others or ourselves naturally, without force, that we've forgotten to trust ourselves and to trust the forces of life that created us.

Ultimately, you get to choose. The choice will come down to answering one question for yourself: "Are you living a life worth living?"

Regardless of your answer, the choice I am giving you doesn't cost anything other than the struggle and burden you've been experiencing in life. If you're feeling anything other than enlivened and drawn to action in your life naturally, you're creating something, but it is not a way of life where good things happen naturally for people.

If something I've said conjures up an image for you and a feeling of "Oh, I wouldn't want to live like that," then whatever the image, it is not the new paradigm. Does it make sense that the new paradigm would require you to live in a way that you find distasteful? There is no "either/or"—that is, it's not "Either I get all the things that I really want to be happy *or* a way of

111

life where good things happen naturally for people." Those two things are one and the same, and to the extent that you see them in conflict, you are not creating a way of life where good things happen naturally for people. The things you love about your life, the things important to you, the things you want to pursue in life—all those things can come along for the ride, but if they do, they'll come along as an outcome of design, because they are necessary to live a life where good things happen naturally for people.

This idea, more than anything else, will be your compass as you move forward to create the new paradigm. If you are not authentically experiencing joy and freedom, you are creating something, but it is not the new paradigm. Somehow, someway, you are focused on an outcome of past design, and it has become a barrier to creating what you want. Rather than be "right," you must keep questioning your thinking.

We spend so much of our time debating the "right" way to live or the "right" way to solve our problems. If you ask most people, they wouldn't be opposed to a peaceful world without poverty, war, and hunger, where all people are able to get the things they want and need. So, for the most part, we are all in agreement on the ultimate outcomes. People in families and organizations generally agree on the outcomes. Parents want their children to be happy, and their children want to be happy (and want their parents to be happy). People at all levels in an organization care about and want the organization to thrive. We spend so much time, though, debating and struggling over the pathway, but the struggle is only given by a belief that we have to work hard to have good things, that we live in a world where there isn't enough of the things people need to live healthy, satisfying lives. This doesn't mean that everyone on the planet will have a big-screen television—we may discover that life and its limitations has something to say about that. But are we ready to settle on what we've created as the "right" way to live?

"I knew it," you may find yourself thinking. "I knew that somehow there was going to be sacrifice involved."

Actually, there isn't.

Think of it this way: you likely don't play with your baby toys, but you don't feel as if you've given up something. You simply don't play with them because you outgrew those things. You gave them up naturally, as a part of growing up. That's how it will seem to you with respect to many of the things in your life. The impetus to want them, protect them, fight for them, cling to them, or even work hard for them simply won't be there. Why? Because a way of life designed so good things happen naturally for people is going to be designed to give you (and others) the things you really want and need to be satisfied. If you think you're designing a way of life where good things happen naturally for people *and* you're not feeling like you're getting what you want and need, then again, you're designing *something*, but it's not the new paradigm. So yes, you might choose to no longer pursue certain things in your life, but it won't be because I dictated to you the "right" way to live. It won't be because I told you that a television, or a million dollars, or a new Lexus is not good for you or that it is not part of a way of life where good things happen naturally for people. By creating a way of life where good things happen naturally for people, whatever is required to live that way of life will be created (or will remain from what we've already created), and whatever isn't necessary will be phased out naturally.

Sacrifice—and by extension, not creating what we really want—is a result of not understanding the creative process. As we've seen, we often create what we want and what we don't want simultaneously. We want peace, but we don't want peace at the expense of our own comfort or safety. We want hunger and poverty to be eradicated from the planet, but we don't want others' ability to eat and provide for themselves to jeopardize our ability to eat and provide for ourselves. We know the world we want to live in, but we sit at the table—in our homes and in our governments and organizations—and we debate a course of action to find the "right" way. And the best we often can hope for is that we can "agree to disagree," implying that we have different opinions of how we should proceed.

The thing is … it's not opinion. It's creation. As we begin

to understand that our thinking today is an outcome of past design, and how we think today both got us here today and is insufficient for us to move forward and create the world we really want to live in tomorrow, then what emerges is the possibility for us to come together and focus on what it is we really want—the eradication of all those things we don't want anymore, without a cost to anyone.

Or more appropriately said, what we really want is to live a fulfilling life. What we want is to live in a way of life where good things happen naturally for all people.

Simply put, we want to live a life worth living.

Thank you for taking this journey with me.

I wish you well.

I wish you a life worth living.